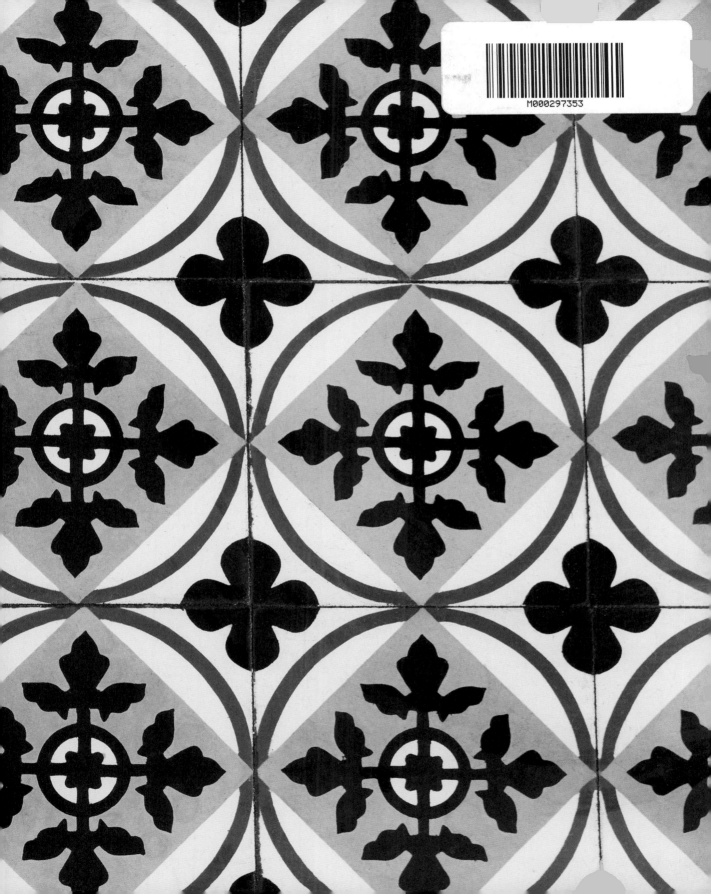

M000297353

modern
sourdough

modern sourdough

**SWEET AND SAVOURY
RECIPES FROM
MARGOT BAKERY**

michelle eshkeri

PHOTOGRAPHY BY
PATRICIA NIVEN

WHITE LION
PUBLISHING

CONTENTS

INTRODUCTION

I was born in Manchester and grew up in Australia, before moving to London when I was 22. I found my community and started my family in North London. I opened Margot for the same reason I started baking bread at home, because there was nowhere in easy travelling distance for me to buy good bread for my family. I found a dilapidated ex-post office around the corner from my home and set about convincing the landlord to trust me with its reinvention and persuading lenders to provide money. I learned one step at a time about installing three phase electricity and how to lay out a bakery and a shop and manage suppliers, employment law, VAT and baking in large volumes amongst a hundred other lessons.

The baking at Margot is not always easy to define: our influences range from the fresh bold flavours found in Australian food, comforting recipes from the north of England to traditional Italian baking techniques and Polish and Hungarian fillings; we bake for both Jewish and Christian festivals. Sourdough doesn't belong to a single culture or country and in opening the bakery as a self-taught baker and as a woman, I believe that I have something worthwhile to offer in baking bread – as much as a bakery with a long illustrious history or a baker using a one hundred year old sourdough starter. A lack of experience or one's gender or a lack of equipment need not be a barrier to baking bread. Our bread is not always perfect, but my priority has always been, and will always be, quality. And with passion and determination I sincerely believe anyone can make good bread.

People often comment on the amount of patience it must take to be a baker as though we were a serene and contented type. I don't disagree that to bake is good for the soul, but it is also for hungry and impatient people who have discovered the satisfaction of creating, holding and consuming their best work in hours or at most days. Baking feeds your body and soul and usually welcomes positive responses from those who receive the results. Gratification is fairly immediate and as one batch ends the next is close behind or already underway, ready for the next thrill. I have learned my craft through trial and error, from experiments and conversations in person and online; collecting and discarding ideas as I went. There is not only one way to make bread and there are as many ways to make good bread as there are bakers. The pleasure of sourdough is that all but the biggest disasters are usually edible and you learn something with each bake. It may not be perfect or beautiful but it will almost certainly be delicious.

The recipes in this book can be followed as they are but please do also consider them a starting point: endless variations are possible. You can adjust the processes and experiment with different quantities and flavour additions. I am including the formulas that we use in the bakery and they have evolved based on opening hours and shift patterns as well as my own preference for bread and pastries made with a mature starter and a long cold final proof. It is a book of the Margot bread as it has evolved from its beginnings in my own kitchen. It isn't flashy or fancy, I always choose flavour and practicality over appearance. Often the most beautiful bread lacks flavour and spectacular oven spring can mean under-hydrated, under-fermented bread. Style is not more important than substance at Margot but there is a sweet spot where the two intersect and a beautiful and delicious bread remains the goal for all of us every day.

One of the most challenging aspects of sourdough is in working with sweet doughs. The usual process is much slower than when one uses commercial yeast and structure and time scales are wildly different. It was the focus of some of my most extensive experiments even before opening the bakery and we are, though I hope not for too long, one of the few bakeries in the UK which naturally leaven all our bread and vienoisserie with sourdough. It is more difficult from a production and logistical point of view but I believe despite the time it takes and trouble it can cause that the flavour is exceptional. Complex and varied and delicious; even when it is perfectly sweet, it has a tang and depth that is like no other sweet bread in the world.

For all the difficult moments, mistakes I have made and stressful days and nights involved in opening a business, the extraordinary pleasure I get from customers saying how much they enjoy our produce and the pleasure of watching the shop fill with people who have come to their local bakery is so incredibly satisfying. It's a community – firstly of the bakers and the team who work in the kitchen and front of house. They have inspired and challenged me and I have learned so much from each person I have worked with. It's also a community of neighbours and bread lovers, locals and those who visit the UK from all parts of the world and make time to come to see us. I'm still learning and get through by seeking the expertise of others, learning from mistakes and a good dose of intuition to continue our growth and to allow innovation. It's a work in progress and a personal, complicated journey while also standing alone and separate from me. This book then, is a record of the journey to Margot and of the recipes I love and a record of a place I helped to create. It captures the essence of the journey and the recipes that we bake and work on every day.

BREAD

MAKING A SOURDOUGH STARTER

Sourdough is the name given to a natural process of fermentation used most often to leaven bread and other doughs. It is an ancient process that at its most simple involves mixing flour, water and salt and waiting hours or days and then baking the mix.

The act of combining flour and water and leaving it to ferment will create a starter that provides the natural leavening for the dough. Wheat or rye flours are commonly used to make a starter and the yeast and bacteria that are naturally present on the grain are harnessed, concentrated and trained to behave in a predictable way.

Creating and maintaining the starter through regular refreshments during its establishment and thereafter, means that a loaf of bread is always within your reach. A vigorous starter will produce a lighter loaf and more satisfying results. If the starter is happy, the bread will be good.

HOW TO MAKE A SOURDOUGH STARTER

MAKES 100g (3½ oz)

Ready in 8–21 days

1kg (2¼ lb) whole wheat flour
water

A basic sourdough starter can be made with any wheat or rye flour – it doesn't have to be fancy or expensive. I find wholegrain and organic flour is best as you are trying to harness the natural organisms present on the grain, so the more the better, although it isn't absolutely necessary. Tap water is perfectly fine for sourdough starters and doughs – you can use very slightly warm water if the weather is cold and you want to give your starter or dough a boost.

The number of days it takes to make the starter will vary so the times in the chart on pages 14–15 should be used as a guide. In warmer weather the starter will ferment faster in which case go with the lower end of the scale or even less time and the reverse is true in very cold weather or if your kitchen is especially cold.

A starter made with white wheat flour may take an additional 1–2 days longer to ferment and establish but should be ready to use by the end of 21 days.

Follow these important points when making your starter:

- **Leave the starter in a warm place** During summer the kitchen work surface is fine, in winter choose a constantly warm area – on top of the fridge, for example. Keep at room temperature throughout and once your starter is ready to include in recipes, refer to How to store your starter.
- **Use a clean jar** Transfer the starter to a clean jar every day at the beginning of the process. It is best to use a Kilner jar or a large jar with a cloth on top secured with an elastic band. Avoid jars with screw top lids for storing sourdough starters as they don't allow the gases to escape For details of changing jars later on in the process see Once the Starter is Established (see page 16).
- **Mixing the starter** Always mix the starter with clean hands or a clean spoon until all the flour is hydrated and no dry patches remain.

STEP BY STEP GUIDE TO MAKING A STARTER	DAY	METHOD	INGREDIENTS TO BE ADDED
	1	Place ingredients in a jar, stir, cover with a cloth, secure with an elastic band and leave in a warm place.	25g (1 oz) whole wheat flour 25g (1 oz) water
	2	After 24 hours transfer the Day 1 mixture into a clean jar and stir in the Day 2 ingredients. Cover as before and leave in a warm place.	25g (1 oz) whole wheat flour 25g (1 oz) water
	3	After 24 hours transfer the Day 2 mixture into a clean jar and stir in the Day 3 ingredients. Cover as before and leave in a warm place. There may now be some bubbles of activity as the yeast and bacteria multiply. If not, then find a warmer spot and repeat the day 2 process for an additional 1–2 days	25g (1 oz) whole wheat flour 25g (1 oz) water
	4	After 24 hours weigh out 20g (¾ oz) of the starter from Day 3 and place in a clean jar. Discard the remaining Day 3 starter. Add the Day 4 ingredients into the jar. Mix until well combined with no dry patches of flour. It will be a fairly stiff dough. Cover as before and leave in a warm place.	50g (1¾ oz) whole wheat flour 30g (1 oz) water
	5	Weigh out 20g (¾ oz) of the starter from Day 4 and place in a clean jar. Discard the remaining Day 4 starter. Add the Day 5 ingredients into the jar. Mix until well combined with no dry patches of flour. It will be a fairly stiff dough. Cover as before and leave in a warm place.	50g (1¾ oz) whole wheat flour 30g (1 oz) water

DAY	METHOD	INGREDIENTS TO BE ADDED
6	Weigh out 20g (¾ oz) of the starter from Day 5 and place in a clean jar. Discard the remaining starter. Add the Day 6 ingredients into the jar. Mix until well combined with no dry patches of flour. It will be a fairly stiff dough. Cover and leave in a warm place.	50g (1¾ oz) whole wheat flour 30g (1 oz) water
7	Weigh out 20g (¾ oz) of the starter from Day 6 and place in a clean jar. Discard the remaining Day 6 starter. Add the Day 7 ingredients into the jar. Mix until combined with no dry patches of flour. It will be a fairly stiff dough. Cover and leave in a warm place.	50g (1¾ oz) whole wheat flour 30g (1 oz) water
8–14	If the starter has at least doubled in volume and has visible bubbles 12 hours after the last refreshment then it may be ready to use for baking. If it seems alive but not moving much, continue the same pattern of discarding and refreshing 24 hours apart until at least doubled in volume 12 hours after refreshment. Use slightly warm water and move the starter to a warmer place if it seems inactive or is not increasing in volume every day.	50g (1¾ oz) whole wheat flour 30g (1 oz) water
15–21	If your starter does not seem strong enough, repeat the process for days 8–14. Once you have a good, strong starter you can be more flexible about storage and maintenance and expect consistent results when you bake.	50g (1¾ oz) whole wheat flour 30g (1 oz) water

ONCE THE STARTER IS ESTABLISHED

If you are refreshing your starter every day it isn't necessary to change the jar every day once the starter is established. However, I find that it is best to change the jar every 2–3 days to avoid any build up of old starter on the sides or contamination with less friendly bacteria that may negatively impact the starter.

MAINTAINING A STARTER AND COLD STORAGE BETWEEN BAKES

If you bake regularly then it may be most practical to keep your starter at room temperature. A refreshment once every 24 hours when you are often in the kitchen is not time consuming and the upside is you are never more than a few hours from being able to mix a dough. There is a difference though between keeping a starter alive and having it at its peak for mixing dough. A refreshment once in 24 hours, or even, should you forget to refresh it, after 36 or 48 hours, will be enough to keep it alive. However, to have a vigorous starter ready for baking, a morning refreshment on day 1 followed by an evening refreshment 12 hours or so later will allow you to mix a dough on day 2.

If you go on holiday or bake once a week or perhaps once a month then it makes sense to keep your starter in the fridge. Refresh it as normal and when it is at its peak i.e. at the point you would usually use it to mix a dough, pop it in the fridge. It will be fine for weeks potentially – it depends on how cold your fridge is. My policy is to refresh a refrigerated starter every week, if possible, but not to leave it for any longer than three weeks. It's important to regularly refresh the starter, even if you're not going to use it – refreshment will wake it up before it goes dormant once more.

BAKING WITH A SOURDOUGH STARTER

If you're refreshing your starter in order to bake make sure you reserve a small amount, even just 20–25g (¾–1 oz), so that you can refresh it for future bakes. The quantity of starter specified in the recipes in the book, is often more than is needed. This is because some volume is lost during fermentation and some will stick to the jar, the spoon and your hands – it's always better to have slightly more than you need. A little extra also allows you to retain a small portion to maintain and keep alive for another bake. Take care not to use it all in the dough and you can develop a system for the longevity of your starter. I usually have some in the fridge and some on the work surface so that if one were to be lost, the other remains.

PREPARING THE STARTER TO USE IN RECIPES
The starter that is used for the first stage of all the recipes is a starter that has been refreshed as detailed below.

If the starter has been refrigerated
Remove the starter from the fridge and add 5–10g (¼ oz) of it to 30g (1 oz) water in a clean jar, mix briefly and then add 50g (1¾ oz) flour. Discard the rest of the unused starter. Mix with a spoon or your hand until no dry patches of flour remain. Leave to ferment for 24 hours at room temperature. Repeat the refreshment and allow to ferment for approximately 12 hours at room temperature before using for stage 1 of the recipes.

If the starter has not been refrigerated
Take a clean jar and add 5–10g (¼ oz) of the starter to 30g (1 oz) water, mix briefly in the jar and then add 50g (1¾ oz) flour. Discard the rest of the unused starter. Mix until no dry patches of flour remain. Leave to ferment for approximately 12 hours at room temperature before using for stage 1 of the recipes.

USING BAKER'S PERCENTAGES
Baker's percentages are an enormously useful tool when you are practiced at making bread and want to understand how you can adjust a recipe through changes to the type or quantities of ingredients. An experienced baker can look at a formula and know from the relationship between the flour and the water or the starter and the flour what type of bread to expect.

When you look at other recipes or want to convert yeast based-recipes to make a sourdough version, you will find bread formulas are given in one of two ways. When baking at home, I prefer to use the method that gives each of the ingredients a percentage, including the flour and water in the starter. This makes the relationship between all ingredients easier to understand. For example, the amount of fermented flour in the starter may be 15% and the flour in the mix is 85% making a combined total of 100%. The required weight of the salt can be worked out based on the total flour. The same principle applies for the hydration which will also take into account the water in the starter.

Salt helps develop the gluten in the dough but most importantly makes it taste of something. When using baker's percentages, a rule of thumb is 1.8–2% of salt to 100% flour – though this can be changed to suit personal tastes. Slightly more salt may be needed for breads with added seeds or grains and slightly less for sweeter doughs. Bread without enough salt will taste flat; salt brings it to life.

When working out the hydration or amount of liquid to be used in a recipe, this should include the water in the starter. Water can be changed at whim when baking – it is always up to you and what you think the dough needs. I have learnt the value in making sure there is enough water in a dough, even if it is harder to manage. A normal range of total water in a formula in relation to total flour could be anywhere from 60 to 90% depending on the style of bread and any additions. Bread with seeds or dried fruit added often requires more water. Comparing the quantites used in a recipe is a good way to understand how flour, salt and water interact with each other and how baker's percentages work. Here the total hydration is 77.8%.

INGREDIENT	AMOUNT	PERCENTAGE
Flour	500g (1 lb 2 oz)	89%
Water	400g (14 oz)	71%
Salt	10g (¼ oz)	1.8%
Flour in starter	62.5g (2½ oz)	11%
Water in starter	37.5g (1½ oz)	6.8%

Most bread formulas in the book use a starter at 60% or 80% hydration. A starter at 100% hydration is sometimes used to build the starter for sweet doughs. If you can understand baker's percentages, you can change a formula to suit your flour or location or personal preferences without running the risks that come with trial and error – it allows you to understand the very structure of your process.

NOTES ON FLOUR

I recommend using a flour with around 12% protein content for the recipes in the book. This may be 'plain' flour rather than 'bread' flour; the protein content is listed with the nutritional information on the pack. A softer flour gives a softer crumb; you can use bread or plain flour but it isn't necessary to use extra strong flour. I like to use organic flour but you can make bread from almost any flour.

NOTES ON TEMPERATURE

The main way to control the fermentation of your dough is to adjust the water temperature when mixing as you have less control over room temperature and other variables. You will learn to read the dough from experience and can extend or reduce the bulk time time as needed. Aim for a final dough temperature of 28ºC (82ºF) just as you finish mixing the dough and around 26ºC (79ºF) in warm weather. A probe thermometer is a useful baking tool for consistent results.

THE DOUGH PROCESS

The following steps need to be completed as you make the dough.

THE AUTOLYSE STAGE

This is the stage where the flour and water for the dough are mixed together, prior to adding the starter. The purpose of the autolyse stage is to allow the gluten to begin to develop gently with minimal effort or friction. By adding water to the flour, proteins begin to form and so less mixing time and folds are required later in the process.

The autolyse stage can help with timing: it can be left out if it suits your schedule however, it can also be extended – as there is no starter in the mix it won't over ferment. It can last for several hours or even overnight if you get called away before you can complete the mixing process. At Margot, we find extending the autolyse particularly beneficial for breads with larger proportions of whole grain flour.

MIXING THE DOUGH

It is possible to make bread without a mixer. It takes a bit more time, but the results are just as good. The technique for developing the gluten in sourdough breads with relatively high proportions of water is different to the more familiar and traditional techniques for yeast doughs.

The most important thing is to never add any more flour to the dough – not on your hands or the bench. Use wet hands or a little oil in the bowl instead. The flour in the recipes is already in correct proportion to the water and salt, if you add extra flour to the dough at any stage it will not hydrate properly and you will have heavy, dry bread. Trust the process and as the dough develops and the gluten strengthens with the autolyse, mixing and then folds, the dough loses its sticky quality and becomes strong and smooth without the need for any extra flour. It will be stickiest at the start – this is normal and doesn't indicate problems.

It makes sense to develop the dough in a bowl as it is less messy but it can be done in any way you prefer including on a work surface.

TO MIX BY HAND IN THE BOWL

1. Once the starter and salt have been added and squeezed through the dough, grip the bowl with one hand and use the other one to reach under it and take a handful of the dough from the bottom of the bowl. Bring it up and over to the middle point of the top of the dough.

2. Repeat the process turning the bowl a little with each movement, so that you move around the dough evenly, pulling it up and stretching it onto itself in a circular motion. You don't have to be too firm or pull very hard, it is a relatively gentle process. Keep going until the dough feels stronger and it starts to pull away from you when you try to stretch it. This will usually take 5-10 minutes when making bread.

3. Stop at this point and begin the rest period suggested in the recipe before making the series of folds that complete the bulk fermentation.

BULK FERMENTATION OF THE DOUGH

This is the period where the dough is left to rest after mixing and before shaping. If the dough requires folds, they will be completed during this stage. The aim is for the dough to increase in volume by 20–30%. It can take place at room temperature or partly at room temperature and partly in the fridge. The times given in recipes are based on an ambient room temperature of around 20–22ºC (68–71ºF). If room temperature is above or below this then timings may need to be adjusted accordingly. In the middle of winter you would expect the dough to require more time and on a warm summer day, less time. The amount of time needed also varies according to the type of dough – enriched doughs such as Challah (see page 46) take longer – and how much starter the dough contains in proportion to the flour.

It's important to watch the dough at this stage and this comes with experience. If you think it can take more time and it looks or feels cold and heavy it usually can and conversely if you see it escaping the bowl early on in the process move to the next stage promptly. By the time it is shaped you don't want a bubbling over-fermented mass but a strong and lively dough that is moving but still has enough vigour to complete the next stage.

FOLDING THE DOUGH

It helps to think of the dough as having four sides when folding (even if it is in a round bowl). Wet one hand while the other holds the container or bowl and reach under the dough and lift it as far as you can without tearing and place the lifted section onto the centre of the dough. Repeat on the other three sides. Four folds should be fine with practice but you can do eight or more if you think it needs it or if you are being very gentle. It is time to stop when you feel resistance in the dough; don't be tempted to tear it or keep going at that point. Then turn the ball of dough over so the bottom is now at the top of the bowl. This helps keep the tension you have just created as the seam is now underneath the weight of the dough.

The dough rests between folds so the gluten can relax. It should become smoother, visibly stronger, less sticky and increasingly hold its shape at the edges with each fold.

PRE-SHAPING THE DOUGH

Turn the dough out onto a clean, unfloured surface with the aid of a dough scraper. Flour your hand and lightly flour the top of the dough but try not to allow any flour to get mixed into the dough or on the underside. Using one hand to hold the dough and your other hand holding a dough scraper, tuck the bottom of the dough under itself where it meets the work surface and move the ball of dough in small circular movements. Try and keep it in a single position rather than moving across the work surface – imagine there is a dot underneath the dough and you are trying to keep it on the dot. You are trying to develop some tension on the top of the ball of dough, which will help with structure in the final loaf. When it feels taut and rounded, place it on a lightly floured surface but do not cover. If you see the dough tearing then stop and let the dough rest.

After 20–30 minutes the dough should have relaxed – ideally it should have rounded edges where the dough meets the work surface. It should have a slight skin on top where it has been exposed to the air.

SHAPING THE DOUGH

Very lightly dust a work surface with flour and turn the dough over onto the flour using a dough scraper to help you lift it cleanly. The top 'skin' side should now be downwards and in contact with the floured work surface and you should have the sticky side facing upwards.

Gently, and without pulling at the dough, fold the bottom third up to the middle like you are folding a letter. Fold in the left edge to the middle and then the right side and finally the top down so all four sides have been folded in, creating a neat parcel.

You now have a roughly square piece of dough in front of you. Starting on the top left corner, take an edge of the dough and take the matching corner from the right side. 'Stitch' the dough down its length three or four times towards you so that you have knitted the left and right side together by taking some dough from each side and connecting them in the middle. It's like doing up buttons on a baby's cardigan! You will have a rectangle of dough in front of you with the short sides at the top and bottom.

For a batard loaf roll the dough away from you from the bottom of the rectangle as if you are rolling up a Swiss roll. You are aiming to have an even piece of dough, uniform in size.

For a round loaf fold the dough on itself towards you, more or less in half, and then turn it over onto an unfloured surface so the seam-side is down on the work surface. Flour your hand and lightly flour the top of the dough then repeat the pre-shaping technique, using a dough scraper, turning the loaf around in a single position until it forms a uniform round shape with some tension. This is quite a tricky technique to master and it takes practice – the first few times you do this you may have the dough sticking to your hands.

Dust the shaped loaf in a mixture of white rice flour and whole wheat flour and place seam-side up in a banneton dusted with rice flour or into a bowl lined with a tea towel generously dusted with rice flour. Proof according to the recipe.

SCORING LOAVES

The classic score we use for the Margot loaf is a single straight line. For a round loaf use a balanced set of lines or patterns so that the loaf can expand evenly.

It is important to score the loaf evenly. Dust the loaf with rice flour, rubbing it over the loaf with your hand – this helps a blade slide through the dough without sticking when you score it and also provides a pleasing contrast with the exposed dough where you have made the cut against the dusted crust of the loaf. Using a baking lame, start from the very edge of the loaf and once the corner of the blade has gone under the skin, have the blade at a 45° angle to the surface of the loaf. Pull it firmly and definitively through the skin at the top of the loaf, about 5mm (¼ in) deep. A sharp knife or even a pair of scissors can also be used to the score the dough.

BAKING INSTRUCTIONS

Baking in a cast iron pot quite closely recreates the conditions in a professional bread oven where the bread is loaded at a high temperature and steam can be added at the touch of a button and allowed to escape at the right moment in the bake. Alternatively bake on a preheated baking tray or stone and add steam to help recreate the ideal baking environment.

BAKING IN A CAST IRON POT

Place a sheet of baking parchment on a work surface. Turn your shaped loaf out onto the paper, seam-side down and the smooth side facing you. Cut the paper roughly around the shape of your loaf, leaving two long pieces of paper on two sides of the loaf to help lower the loaf into the pot. Score the loaf (see Scoring Loaves).

Carefully take the preheated pot out of the oven, lower the loaf in and replace the lid. Put the pot back in the oven and follow the recipe directions to bake the bread. If the base of the loaf is getting too dark, transfer to a baking tray for the final stage of the bake. Bake until it sounds hollow when tapped on the bottom and has a deep brown colour. It won't colour properly until the steam is released when the lid comes off so this last phase of baking is important. Be bold and don't cut this stage short as a fully baked crust means the crumb will be set and have the correct texture – the crust will stay crispy and not soften as soon as it cools. In my experience there is a range of preferences for final loaf colour – one person's burned loaf is another's under baked. I favour a boldly baked loaf!

BAKING ON A TRAY OR STONE WITH STEAM

Place the bread onto the preheated tray or stone and add some water to the roasting tin. Bake the bread following your recipe, removing the water tray for the final third of the cooking time so the bread can colour and crisp up.

COOLING AND STORING BREAD

Allow loaves to cool on a wire rack for at least an hour before slicing. Store the bread wrapped in a clean cloth or greaseproof paper to retain the crispy crust. Never store bread in the fridge or it will stale quickly. Use plastic to preserve freshness for longer but this will be at the expense of the crispy crust.

THE MARGOT

When I opened the bakery we tested several loaves in this style; fairly simple with a whole wheat starter, some rye flour for structure and flavour, and enough water to make a daily loaf that could sit in a kitchen for a day or two or three; suitable for toast, to make a sandwich for lunch or to serve with salad or soup for dinner. It's the most popular loaf at the bakery, our customers ask for it by name and it has become the yardstick by which we measure how good all the products are. If the Margot is happy we are all happy!

Feel free to reduce the water content a little while you get used to handling and shaping the dough and work your way up – 20g (¾ oz) less water will give a firmer, more manageable dough while you master the techniques.

MAKES 1 LOAF
800g (1¾ lb)

Stage 1: Refreshment
70g (2¾ oz) whole wheat flour
42g (1½ oz) water
5g (⅛ oz) whole wheat starter (8–12 hours after last refreshment)

Stage 2: Dough mix
350g (12 oz) strong white flour
40g (1½ oz) wholegrain rye flour
335g (11½ oz) water
8g (¼ oz) sea salt
rice flour, for dusting
sunflower oil, for greasing

1. Place all the stage 1 ingredients in a 500ml (17 fl oz) Kilner jar or container with a lid, mix, cover and leave at room temperature for 12–16 hours

2. Combine the flours and water for stage 2 in a large bowl and mix with a spoon or your hand until no dry patches of flour remain visible. Or, in a free standing mixer fitted with a dough hook, mix for 3 minutes on a low speed and 2 minutes on a medium speed. Scrape down the sides, cover and leave for 30–60 minutes.

3. Add 100g (3½ oz) of the starter to the bowl and squeeze it through the mixture with your hand – use one hand rather than two; at this stage the dough is sticky and you are better off keeping one hand free of dough to hold the bowl. Add the salt and squeeze it through the dough.

4. Develop the dough in the bowl by hand mixing for 5–10 minutes (see Mixing the Dough on pages 19–20). Alternatively you can use a free standing mixer fitted with a dough hook for 2 minutes on a low speed and 3–5 minutes on a medium speed.

5. Use the sunflower oil to grease a large mixing bowl or a rectangular flat bottomed glass or plastic container with a lid and capacity of at least 2 litres (3½ pints). Transfer the dough to the bowl or container, cover and rest for 20 minutes.

6. Fold the dough four times, leaving 20 minutes between each fold, then give the dough an additional hour to rest.

7. Pre-shape the dough following the instructions on page 21.

8. Shape the dough into a batard loaf following the instructions on pages 21–22.

9. Transfer the dough into a banetton and then leave in the fridge for 16–24 hours.

10. Preheat the oven to 240°C/475°F/gas mark 8 for 40 minutes, placing a cast iron pot inside after 20 minutes. Once it is hot, lower the bread into the pot and place the lid on top and return to the oven. Reduce the temperature to 220°C/425°F/ gas mark 7 and bake for 15 minutes, then reduce the oven temperature again to 200°C/400°F/gas mark 6 and bake for a further 15 minutes. Remove the lid and bake for a final 10–15 minutes until it has reached the desired colour (see the Baking Instructions on page 23).

11. Allow to cool for at least an hour before slicing. Store wrapped in cloth or paper to retain the crispy crust. Never store in the fridge or it will stale quickly and only wrap in plastic to preserve freshness for longer, though this will be at the expense of the crispy crust.

BROWN BREAD

This is a baker's loaf; when you eat bread daily you seek depth in the flavours and textures, which is the reason the majority of the breads we make at Margot contain some wholegrain. This loaf holds steady with a little over 50 per cent wholegrain content but we change the flours regularly utilising Khorasan, dark spelt flour and einkorn for variety in the mixing and in the eating. I especially like Khorasan as it has good flavour and structure. We also experiment with different proofing times and hydration and we learn something from this bread with each bake. There is little point including it on the bakery shelves beyond Thursday as at this point in the week resolutions to eat more wholegrains are waning and a tendency to indulge arrives.

MAKES 1 LOAF
900g (2 lb)

Stage 1: Refreshment
70g (2¾ oz) whole wheat flour
42g (1½ oz) water
35g(1¼ oz) wheat starter (8–12 hours after last refreshment)

Stage 2: Dough mix
210g (7½ oz) Khorasan flour
210g (7½ oz) strong white bread flour
365g (12½ oz) water
10g (¼ oz) sea salt
rice flour, for dusting
sunflower oil, for greasing

1. Place all the stage 1 ingredients in a 500ml (17 floz) Kilner jar or container with a lid, mix, cover and leave at room temperature for 4–6 hours.

2. Combine the flour and water for stage 2 in a large bowl and mix with a spoon or your hand until no dry patches of flour remain visible. Or, in a free standing mixer fitted with a dough hook, mix for 2–3 minutes on a low speed. Scrape down the sides, cover and leave for 60 minutes.

3. Add 135g (4¼ oz) of the starter to the bowl and squeeze it through the mix with your hand – use one hand rather than two; at this stage the dough is sticky and you are better off keeping one hand free of dough to hold the bowl. Add the salt and squeeze it through the dough.

4. Develop the dough in the bowl by hand mixing for 5–10 minutes (see Mixing the Dough on pages 19–20). Alternatively, in a free standing mixer fitted with a dough hook, mix for 2 minutes on a low speed and 3 minutes on a medium speed.

5. Use the sunflower oil to grease a large mixing bowl or a rectangular flat bottomed glass or plastic container with a capacity of at least 2 litres (3½ pints). Transfer the dough to the bowl or container, cover and rest for 30 minutes.

6. Fold the dough four times, leaving 30 minutes between each fold (see Folding the Dough on page 20–21). Once you've completed the process, leave the dough to rest for an additional 1–2 hours.

7. Pre-shape the dough following the instructions on page 21. Rest for 30 minutes.

8. Shape the dough into a round loaf following the instructions on pages 21–22.

9. Transfer the dough into a banetton and then leave in the fridge for 16–24 hours.

10. Preheat the oven to 240°C/475°F/gas mark 8 for 40 minutes, placing a cast iron pot inside after 20 minutes. Once it is hot, lower the bread into the pot and place the lid on top and return to the oven. Reduce the temperature to 220°C/425°F/ gas mark 7 and bake for 15 minutes, then reduce the oven temperature again to 200°C/400°F/gas mark 6 and bake for a further 15 minutes. Remove the lid and bake for a final 10–15 minutes until it has reached the desired colour (see the Baking Instructions on page 23 for further details).

NEW YORK LIGHT RYE

The name of this bread refers to the style of bread rather than the rye content. It's the bread to turn to for a sandwich or for toast; imagine the offerings of a New York deli between thick slices. The closer crumb and lower hydration of this loaf compared to The Margot means it can be sliced for sandwiches a couple of hours out of the oven. We fill it with our famous egg mayo with chives, capers and dill, Cheddar and roasted courgette with basil or smoked salmon and cream cheese. This bread taught me two important lessons when the bakery opened; one, that a bread needs a name to make it memorable enough to develop a following of willing buyers, and secondly that caraway divides opinion, so we include the seeds in the loaves only on a Friday.

MAKES 1 LOAF
800g (1 lb)

Stage 1: Refreshment
70g (2½ oz) wholegrain
rye flour
56g (2 oz) water
5g (⅛ oz) wheat or rye
starter (8–12 hours after last
refreshment)

Stage 2: Dough mix
390g (13½ oz) strong white
bread flour
305g (11 oz) water
9g (¼ oz) tsp sea salt
8g (¼ oz) caraway seeds
(optional)
rice flour, for dusting
sunflower oil

1. Place all the stage 1 ingredients in a 500ml (17fl oz) Kilner jar or container with a lid, mix, cover and leave at room temperature for 12 hours. Alternatively use 35g (1¼ oz) of starter instead of 5g (⅛ oz) and leave at room temperature for 4–6 hours.

2. Combine the flour and water for stage 2 in a large bowl and mix with a spoon or your hand until no dry patches of flour remain visible. Or, in a free standing mixer fitted with a dough hook, mix for 2–3 minutes on a low speed. Scrape down the sides, cover and leave for 30–60 minutes.

3. Add 120g (4 oz) of the starter to the bowl and squeeze it through the mixture with your hand – use one hand rather than two; at this stage the dough is sticky and you are better off keeping one hand free of dough to hold the bowl. Add the salt and caraway seeds and squeeze them through the dough.

4. Develop the dough in the bowl by hand mixing for 5–10 minutes (see Mixing the Dough on pages 19–20). Alternatively, in a free standing mixer fitted with a dough hook, mix for 2 minutes on a low speed and 3–5 minutes on a medium speed.

5. Use the sunflower oil to grease a large mixing bowl or a rectangular flat bottomed glass or plastic container with a capacity of at least 2 litres (3½ pints). Transfer the dough to the bowl or container, cover and rest for 30 minutes.

6. Fold the dough twice, leaving 30 minutes between each fold, then give the dough an additional hour to rest.

7. Pre-shape the dough following the instructions on page 21. Rest for 30 minutes.

8. Shape the dough into a batard loaf following the instructions on pages 21–22.

9. Transfer the dough into a banetton and then leave in the fridge for 12–18 hours.

10. Preheat the oven to 240°C/475°F/gas mark 8 for 40 minutes, placing a cast iron pot inside after 20 minutes. Once it is hot, lower the bread into the pot and place the lid on top and return to the oven. Reduce the temperature to 220°C/425°F/gas mark 7 and bake for 15 minutes, then reduce the oven temperature again to 200°C/400°F/gas mark 6 and bake for a further 15 minutes. Remove the lid and bake for a final 10–15 minutes until it has reached the desired colour (see the Baking Instructions on page 23).

GERONIMO

I do love a seeded loaf and the five–seeded Geronimo, named for its strength-giving properties and spectacular oven spring, is a firm favourite with our customers, too. I rarely bring it home as my children do not yet appreciate seeds in their bread, preferring The Margot, a baguette or a slice of challah for the most part. Toasting the seeds brings out their flavour more fully, a technique I borrowed in the early days at the bakery from Jeffrey Hamelman whose book *Bread: A Baker's Book of Techniques and Recipes* is in many ways the bible of baking – his recipes can easily be reworked and adapted as they function alone or as templates for experimentation on a small or large scale, and the breadth of his baking knowledge makes it a valuable reference for any baker.

MAKES 1 LOAF
800g (1¾ lb)

Stage 1: Refreshment
60g (2½ oz) whole wheat flour
36g (1½ oz) water
5g (⅛ oz) wheat starter (8–12 hours after last refreshment)

Stage 1: Soaker
8g (¼ oz) chia seeds
20g (¾ oz) flax seeds
83g (3¼ oz) water

Stage 2: Dough mix
280g (10 oz) strong white bread flour
38g (1½ oz) wholegrain rye flour
243g (9 oz) water
35g (1¼ oz) sunflower seeds
25g (1 oz) sesame seeds
10g (¼ oz) pumpkin seeds
8g (¼ oz) sea salt
rice flour, for dusting
sunflower oil, for greasing

1. Place the stage 1 ingredients in a 500ml (17 fl oz) Kilner jar or container with a lid, mix, cover and leave at room temperature for 10–12 hours.

2. At the same time as the starter is prepared, combine the seeds and cold water for in a 200ml (7 fl oz) container. Cover and leave at room temperature.

3. The following day: combine the flours and water for stage 2 plus the seed soaker in a large bowl and mix with a spoon or your hand until no dry patches of flour remain visible. Or, in a free standing mixer fitted with a dough hook, mix for 2–3 minutes on a low speed. Scrape down the sides, cover and leave for 30–60 minutes.

4. Preheat the oven to 180ºC/350ºF/ gas mark 4. Place the stage 2 seeds on a baking tray and bake for 5–10 minutes, until fragrant and turning golden brown at the edges. Set aside to cool.

5. Add 90g (3¼ oz) of the starter to the bowl and squeeze it through the mixture with your hand – use one hand rather than two; at this stage the dough is sticky and you are better off keeping one hand free of dough to hold the bowl. Add the salt and squeeze it through the dough.

6. Develop the dough in the bowl by hand mixing for 5–10 minutes (see Mixing the

Dough on pages 19–20). Alternatively, in a free standing mixer fitted with a dough hook, mix for 2 minutes on a low speed and 3–5 minutes on a medium speed. Add the seeds in the last 2 minutes of mixing.

7. Use the sunflower oil to grease a large mixing bowl or a rectangular flat bottomed glass or plastic container with a capacity of at least 2 litres (3½ pints). Transfer the dough to the bowl or container, cover and rest for 30 minutes.

8. Fold the dough four times, leaving 30 minutes between each fold, then give the dough an additional hour to rest.

9. Pre-shape the dough following page 21.

10. Shape the dough into a batard loaf following the instructions on pages 21–22.

11. Transfer the dough into a banetton and then leave in the fridge for 12–18 hours.

12. Preheat the oven to 240°C/475°F/gas mark 8 for 40 minutes, placing a cast iron pot inside after 20 minutes. Once it is hot, lower the bread into the pot and place the lid on top and return to the oven. Reduce the temperature to 220ºC/425ºF/ gas mark 7 and bake for 25 minutes, then reduce the oven temperature again to 200ºC/400ºF/gas mark 6 and bake for a further 15 minutes. Remove the lid and bake for a final 10–15 minutes.

BRIOCHE

The brioche dough forms the basis for our famous sourdough babka as well as our cinnamon buns. The structure is provided by the butter so that when the dough has been chilled it is firm and malleable and can be rolled out and shaped. It does like warmth during the whole process and if it doesn't get a chance to ferment properly in the initial bulk stage, no amount of time or warmth will persuade it to rise during the final proof. Developing a dough this rich that is leavened only with sourdough was a challenge and took time, patience and many disasters. There is contrast and complexity with the tang of sour alongside the sweet, rich buttery flavour and it stays soft for days. It is a very special dough and I hope it is of interest to other bakers.

MAKES 9–12 BUNS

Stage 1: Refreshment
30g (1 oz) strong white flour
30g (1 oz) water
15g (½ oz) wheat starter (8–12 hours after last refreshment)

Stage 2: Refreshment
100g (3½ oz) strong white flour
60g (2½ oz) water
25g (1 oz) caster sugar

Stage 3: Dough mix
354g (12¼ oz) strong white flour plus extra for dusting rolls
212g (7½ oz) whole egg
57g (2¼ oz) caster sugar
7g (¼ oz) sea salt
212g (7½ oz) unsalted butter, chilled and cut into 2.5cm (1 in) cubes
sunflower oil, for greasing
beaten egg, to glaze
pinch of salt

1. Place all the stage 1 ingredients in a 1 litre (1¾ pint) Kilner jar or container with a lid, mix, cover and leave at warm room temperature for 8–12 hours.

2. Place the stage 2 ingredients plus 50g (2 oz) of the stage 1 mix in a 1 litre (1¾ pint) Kilner jar or container with a lid. Mix, cover and leave at warm room temperature for 12–16 hours.

3. Combine the flour and egg for stage 3 and 198g (7 oz) of the starter in the bowl of a free standing mixer fitted with a dough hook; mix for 7–8 minutes on a low speed. Scrape down the sides, mix on a medium speed for 5 minutes. Cover and leave for 30 minutes.

4. Add the sugar and salt to the bowl and mix for 5 minutes on a low speed and another 5 minutes on a medium speed.

5. Add the butter, piece by piece, on a low speed with the mixer running. Allow each piece to be absorbed into the dough before adding the next one. Scrape down the sides regularly. Mix for another 10–20 minutes after the butter has been added. The exact length of time will depend on the power of your mixer and you may find that you need to mix for longer. The dough is ready when you can stretch it with your fingers into a thin, transparent window and a hole poked in the window has clean, rather than jagged edges.

6. Use the sunflower oil to grease a large mixing bowl or a rectangular flat bottomed glass or plastic container with a capacity of at least 2 litres (3½ pints). Transfer the dough to the bowl or container, cover and allow to rest for 3–4 hours in a warm place at around 24ºC (208ºF). A preheated oven switched off with a dish of warm water inside works well.

7. The dough won't rise much during this stage but it allows the yeast and bacteria to gain sufficient strength to complete the final proof. Add 1–2 folds if you feel the dough lacks strength.

8. Transfer the dough to the fridge to chill for 1–2 hours or until firm enough to handle easily.

9. Line a 20cm (8 in) square tin with baking parchment. Divide the dough, by weight, into 9 equal pieces (approximately 110g (3¾ oz) each). Dust the top of a piece with flour and with the base of the piece of dough touching the unfloured work surface make small circular motions with your cupped hand over the dough. The dough should start to form a ball with a smooth top. Place in 3 rows of 3 in the tin.

10. Proof the shaped dough for 16–24 hours in a warm place at around 24ºC (208ºF).

continued overleaf

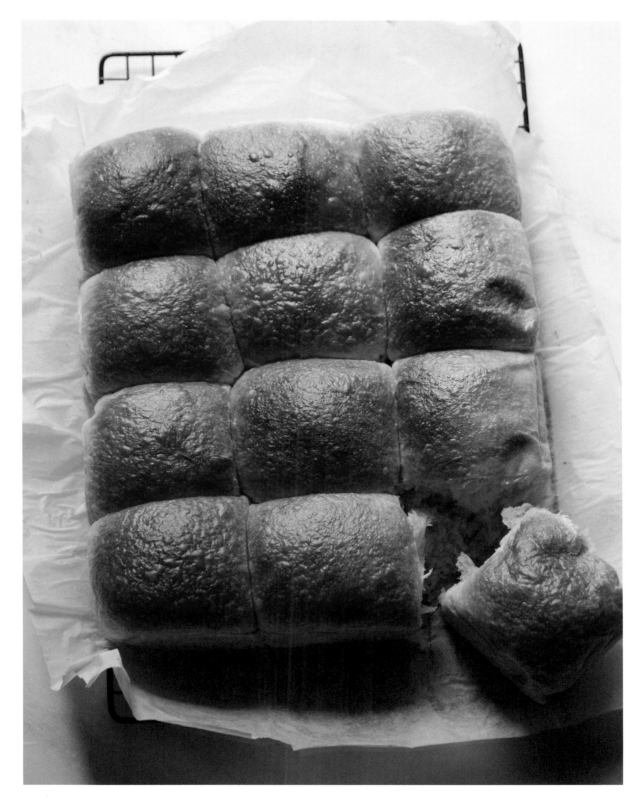

11. Twenty minutes before baking, preheat the oven to 200ºC/400ºF/gas mark 6. Place a metal roasting tin in the oven, to preheat.

12. Glaze the buns with beaten egg and a pinch of salt.

13. When the bread is ready to be baked, pour 100–200ml (3½–7 fl oz) water into the preheated roasting tin and then bake the brioche for 15 minutes. Remove the tin of water and reduce the temperature to 180ºC/350ºF/gas mark 4 and bake for a further 15–20 minutes. The brioche is baked when the internal temperature is 98ºC (208ºF) and a skewer inserted into the centre comes out clean.

MIXING BRIOCHE BY HAND

I don't recommend making brioche by hand though with enough time and energy it could be done. Borrow a mixer off a friend for a few days if you want to give it a try but don't otherwise want or need a mixer in your kitchen permanently! If medium speed seems too much for your mixer, a lower speed will be fine; just extend mixing times.

BAKING THE DOUGH IN A COUPLE OF DAYS?

If you want to make the dough in advance and bake it in 2–3 days, it is better to shape the dough on the day it is mixed while it is still slightly pliable and then chill it in the fridge in the baking tin until you are ready for the final proof. The dough gets increasingly sour with each day it is not baked so 3 days is usually the maximum I would recommend.

FOCACCIA

At Margot we make focaccia to use up ingredients like fruit, vegetables and cheese. The flavour of focaccia dough is at its very best after three days in the fridge; it still has enough structure to be light when baked but it has acquired depth and is softer for the additional fermentation. No advanced baking skills are needed here other than a light touch. Imagine you are playing the piano when you take the dough to the edges of the tin.

MAKES 1 FOCACCIA
1kg (2¼ lb)

Stage 1: Refreshment
10g (¼ oz) strong white flour
10g (¼ oz) water
5g (⅛ oz) wheat starter (8–12 hours after its last refreshment)

Stage 2: Refreshment
33g (1¼ oz) strong white flour
20g (¾ oz) water
8g (¼ oz) caster sugar

Stage 3: Dough mix
525g (1 lb 2½ oz) strong white flour
369g (12¾ oz) water
65g (2½ oz) extra virgin olive oil
11g (¼ oz) sea salt
7g (¼ oz) caster sugar
olive oil, for greasing

Topping
40g (1½ oz) extra virgin olive oil
40g (1½ oz) water
2 crushed garlic cloves
8–10g (¼ oz) chopped rosemary or 10–15g (¼–½ oz) chopped thyme
sea salt, for sprinkling

1. Mix all the stage 1 ingredients in a Kilner jar or container with a lid, with a capacity of at least 500ml (17fl oz). Cover and leave at room temperature for 8–12 hours.

2. Mix all the stage 2 ingredients into the jar or container containing the stage 1 starter, cover and leave at warm room temperature for 8–10 hours.

3. Combine the flour and water for stage 3 in a large bowl with 63g (2½ oz) of the starter, the extra virgin olive oil, salt and sugar. Mix with a spoon or your hand until no dry patches of flour remain visible and then mix in the bowl for 5–8 minutes. Or, in a free standing mixer fitted with a dough hook, mix for 2 minutes to combine ingredients and then 3 minutes on a medium speed. The gluten won't fully develop at this stage and it won't be completely smooth, it will continue to develop with the folds.

4. Use the olive oil to grease a large mixing bowl or a rectangular flat bottomed glass or plastic container with a capacity of at least 2 litres (3½ pints). Transfer the dough to the bowl or container, cover and rest for 30 minutes.

5. Fold the dough four times, leaving 30 minutes between each fold, then give the dough an additional hour to rest.

6. Place the dough in a glass or plastic lidded container with a capacity of at least 2 litres (3½ pints). Cover and place in the fridge for a minimum of 16 hours or for up to 5 days.

7. Five hours before you want to serve the focaccia, line a 24cm (9½ in) square baking tin with baking parchment and grease the base generously with olive oil.

8. Tip the cold dough into the tin, rub a little oil on top and leave it in a warm place for 1–2 hours.

9. With spread fingertips and using both hands, gently push the dough in straight lines following the lines of the tin. It is easiest if your hands are slightly damp or slightly oiled. The goal at this stage is to gently and evenly take the dough to the edges of the tin after the gluten has had a chance to relax.

10. Leave the dough for another 1–2 hours and then repeat the fingertip stretching process. It should easily reach the edges of the tin at this stage but if it doesn't then wait a little longer. Repeat this process again if needed. The dough is ready to bake when it has risen and reached all sides of the tin and there are visible bubbles and it has a light and pillowy appearance.

11. Twenty minutes before baking, preheat the oven to 240°C/475°F/gas mark 8. Place a metal roasting tin in the oven, to preheat.

12. For the topping, combine the olive oil and water and pour over the bread. Sprinkle the dough with the garlic, herbs and sea salt and push the bread down, all over, with your fingertips.

continued overleaf

13. When the focaccia is ready to be baked, pour 100–200ml (3½–7 fl oz) water into the preheated roasting tin. Place the tin with the focaccia in the oven, reduce the temperature to 225°C/425°F/gas mark 7 and bake for 15 minutes. Remove dish of water from the oven and then bake for an additional 10–15 minutes. Check the base of the focaccia – when it is golden, it's ready. Leave to cool in the tin.

14. Allow to cool for at least 30 minutes before cutting and serving. Store any leftovers at room temperature.

ALTERNATIVE TOPPING IDEAS

MUSHROOM, SAGE AND GORGONZOLA

Before baking, push 300g (11 oz) wiped, sliced mushrooms and 8–10 torn sage leaves into the dough. Drizzle with olive oil and season with salt and pepper. Sprinkle over 200g (7 oz) crumbled Gorgonzola for the final 10–15 minutes of baking time.

APPLE, COMTÉ AND THYME

Before baking, wash and thinly slice 2 crunchy eating apples and push into the dough. Scatter young thyme leaves over the apples and drizzle with olive oil. Add 200g (7 oz) roughly sliced Comté for the final 10–15 minutes of baking time. Add picked fresh thyme to serve.

PEACH, GOAT'S CHEESE AND MINT

Before baking, wash and slice 3–4 ripe peaches. Cut into thick wedges and scatter over the dough, pushing them in with your fingers. Add 180g (6¼ oz) soft, mild goat's cheese for the final 10 minutes of baking time. Add a small bunch of washed, fresh mint, roughly torn, after the focaccia has cooled for 30–40 minutes.

RICOTTA, SPRING ONION, CHIVE, PROVOLONE AND PARMESAN

Spread 150g (5 oz) ricotta all over the dough with your hands just before baking. Drizzle with olive oil, season with salt and pepper and add 100g (3½ oz) sliced spring onions and 30g (1 oz) chopped chives, pushing the onion down into the dough with your fingers. Add 100g (3½ oz) cubed provolone and 50g grated Parmesan for the final 10 minutes of baking.

TOMATO AND MOZZARELLA

Spread pizza sauce (see recipe on page 149) on the dough before it goes in the oven; add grated mozzarella or another cheese for the final 10–15 minutes of baking time. Finish with torn basil.

BAGUETTE

When the bakery opened no one really understood what type of bakery it was. To be honest, we didn't know ourselves much of the time in the early days. People would come in and ask for bloomers and soft buns and more surprisingly for croissants and especially for baguettes. Perhaps when a bakery opens around the corner you immediately think of holidays in France where one of the greatest pleasures is buying a fresh baguette everyday.

Over time we added them on weekends and we now sell them every day. They can be challenging but the perfect combination of timing, fermentation and fine scoring can make an extraordinary baguette: crunchy on the outside and light in the middle. The failures taste good too though, so treat these as work in progress and revisit them often. This formula uses an overnight bulk and the baguettes are shaped and baked the following day.

MAKES 3 BAGUETTES
300g (11 oz) each

Stage 1: Refreshment
10g (¼ oz) strong white
bread flour
10g (¼ oz) water
5g (⅛ oz) wheat starter (8–10
hours after last refreshment)

Stage 2: Refreshment
91g (3¼ oz) strong white
bread flour
30g (1 oz) water
1g salt

Stage 3: Dough mix
444g (15½ oz) white bread
flour, plus extra for dusting
353g (12¼ oz) water
9g (¼ oz) sea salt
5g (⅛ oz) malt syrup or dark
brown sugar
sunflower oil, for greasing
rice flour, for dusting

1. Place all the stage 1 ingredients in a 500ml (17fl oz) Kilner jar or container with a lid, mix, cover and leave at warm room temperature for 8–12 hours.

2. Add the flour, water and sugar for stage 2 to the jar containing the stage 1 starter, mix, cover and leave at warm room temperature for 6–8 hours.

3. Combine the flour, water and salt for stage 3 and all of the starter in a large bowl and mix with a spoon or your hand until no dry patches of flour remain visible. Use one hand rather than two; at this stage the dough is sticky and you are better off keeping one hand free of dough to hold the bowl.

4. Develop the dough in the bowl by hand mixing for 5–8 minutes (see Mixing the Dough on pages 19–20). Or, in a free standing mixer fitted with a dough hook, mix for 2–3 minutes on a low speed then 2–3 minutes on a medium speed.

5. Use the sunflower oil to grease a large mixing bowl or a rectangular flat bottomed glass or plastic container with a capacity of at least 2 litres (3 pints). Transfer the dough to the bowl or container, cover and rest for 30 minutes.

6. Fold the dough firmly three times, with 30 minutes between each fold, then give the dough an additional ½ hour to rest.

7. Transfer the dough to the fridge, in the container, for 12–36 hours

8. Divide the dough into 3 x 300g (11 oz) pieces, shape into rounds (see pages 21–22) and place on a lightly floured surface, dusting the top of the rounds with some flour then allowing to rest for 30–40 minutes.

9. Dust 2 tea towels liberally with rice flour and arrange on a tray the intended length of your baguettes.

10. Take a round of dough, it should still be a little cold which helps to get enough tension in the shape, and turn over onto a lightly floured surface so the top, floured side is now touching the work surface. Pull gently into a slight oval shape with one of the longest sides closest to you. Fold the dough from one longer edge into the centre, repeat with the other longer edge so they meet in the middle. Then fold the dough in half so the two long edges meet. Seal the edges by pressing firmly with your fingers to create a seam. Turn the piece of dough so the seam is underneath, touching the surface and

continued overleaf

with lightly floured hands begin to roll out from the centre to the ends with both hands applying even pressure as you roll your hands outwards. Press more firmly at the ends of the baguette so they are a little tapered. They can be long and thin or short and fat as you prefer but it is practical to bear in mind the length of your baking tray when shaping them.

11. Dust a towel generously with rice flour and place seam-side up on the tea towel and arrange the cloth with folds coming up between each baguette; this method allows the baguettes to maintain the shape you have just formed and they support each other during the final proof. The baguettes should not touch each other, only the floured cloth. Dust the baguettes with more rice flour once they are all on the cloths.

12. Leave to prove for 1–2 hours at room temperature.

13. Preheat the oven to 240ºC/475ºF/ gas mark 8. Place a baking tray or baking stone in the oven to preheat and place a metal roasting tin or deep tray in the bottom of the oven.

14. Line a baking sheet (with no sides) with baking parchment. Turn your baguettes out onto the lined baking sheet and score quickly down their length, either with one long cut angled at 45º or 3–5 shorter overlapping cuts.

15. Load the baguettes into the oven as soon as you can after scoring them. Use the tray to transfer them on to the preheated tray or stone on the parchment – this requires a shuffling action, you want to take care to keep your baguettes straight, as they go in the oven, so a short sharp movement to load them in will work best. Pour some water into the preheated tin in the oven, reduce the temperature to 225ºC/425ºF/gas mark 7 and bake for 15 minutes. Remove the tin of water, and bake for an additional 5–10 minutes until the desired colour is reached. Cool on a wire rack.

FINCHLEY STICKS

One of our early attempts to make baguettes resulted in misshapen pieces of dough so ugly and so un-baguette like that they could not be labelled as such. They did taste good though so tongue in cheek and to the great amusement of the staff, we pushed some olives into the dough, baked them and put them out for sale as 'Finchley sticks'. They quickly gained a following, the customers who bought them came back and asked for them by name and so we kept baking them. They appear less often now that we are fairly competent at baguettes but we make them whenever we make ciabatta or have olives to use up and the name lives on for any rustic, long bread stick with olives.

MAKES 3 STICKS
200g (7 oz) each

Stage 1: Refreshment
8g (¼ oz) strong white bread flour
8g (¼ oz) water
4g (⅛ oz) wheat starter (8–10 hours after last refreshment)

Stage 2: Refreshment
43g (1½ oz) strong white bread flour
25g (1 oz) water
10g (¼ oz) caster sugar

Stage 3: Dough mix
289g (10¼ oz) strong white bread flour
239g (8½ oz) water
4g (⅛ oz) caster sugar
6g (¼ oz) sea salt
extra virgin olive oil, for greasing
12 large green pitted olives, halved

1. Place all the stage 1 ingredients in a 500ml (17 fl oz) Kilner jar or container with a lid, mix, cover and leave at warm room temperature for 8–12 hours.

2. Add the flour, water and sugar for stage 2 to the jar containing the stage 1 starter, mix, cover and leave at warm room temperature for 6–8 hours.

3. Combine the flour, water, sugar and salt for stage 3 and 85g (3¼ oz) of starter in a large bowl and mix with a spoon or your hand until no dry patches of flour remain visible. Use one hand rather than two; at this stage the dough is sticky and you are better off keeping one hand free of dough to hold the bowl.

Develop the dough in the bowl by hand mixing for 5–8 minutes (see Mixing the Dough on pages 19–20). Or, in a free standing mixer fitted with a dough hook, mix for 2–3 minutes on a low speed then 2–3 minutes on a medium speed.

4. Use the olive oil to grease a large mixing bowl or a rectangular flat bottomed glass or plastic container with a capacity of at least 2 litres (3 pints). Transfer the dough to the bowl or container, cover and rest for 30 minutes.

5. Firmly fold the dough three times, leaving 30 minutes between each fold, then give the dough an additional 30 minutes to rest.

6. Transfer to the fridge in the container for 12–36 hours

7. Brush your work surface with a thin layer of oil and turn the cold dough out in a single piece onto the surface. Rub the top of your dough with more oil and shape the dough with your hands so you have a rectangle approx. 7.5 x 20cm (3–8 in) Take a dough cutter or knife and cut the rectangle of dough into 3 long pieces 2.5 x 20cm (1–8 in) in size – the oil on top should stop the blade sticking to the dough. The goal is to l eave the structure of the dough as intact as possible.

8. Line a 25–30cm (10–12 in) long tray with baking parchment. Oil your hands and lift your pieces of dough, stretching them as little as possible onto the lined tray. They will stretch a little as you lift them. Push 8 olive halves into each stick as firmly as you can.

continued overleaf

9. Leave to prove for 1–2 hours at room temperature.

10. Preheat the oven to 240ºC/475ºF/gas mark 8. Place a baking tray or baking stone in the oven to preheat and place a metal roasting tin or deep tray in the bottom of the oven.

11. Push the olives into the dough again one more time and then carefully transfer the sticks on their piece of baking parchment onto the preheated oven tray.

12. Pour some water into the preheated tin in the oven, reduce the temperature to 225ºC/425ºF/gas mark 7, close the door and bake for 10 minutes. Remove the tin of water and bake for an additional 5–10 minutes until the desired colour is reached. Leave to cool on a wire rack.

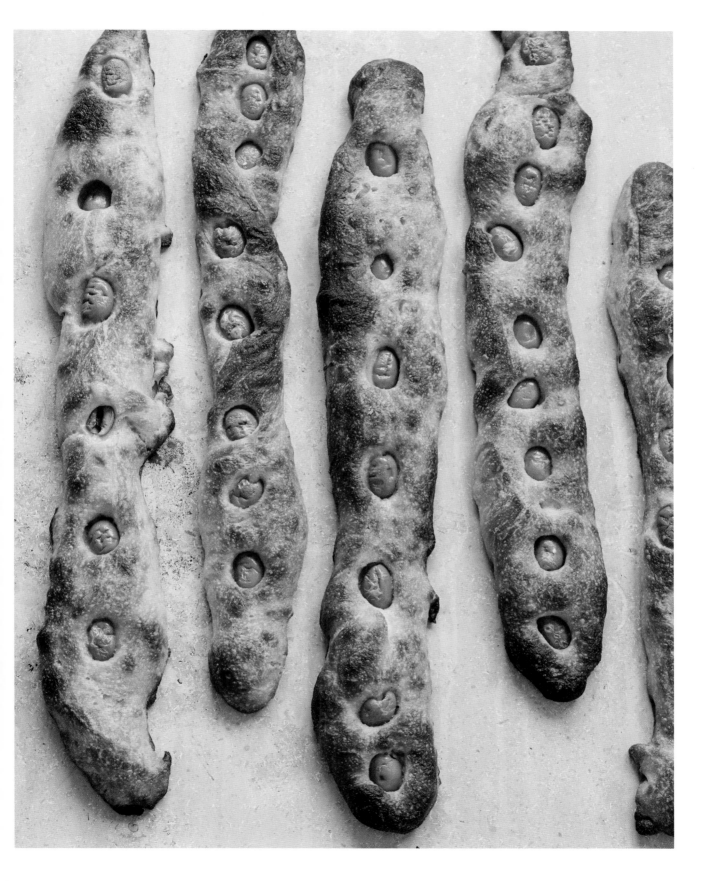

BREAD

CIABATTA

As ciabatta doesn't require shaping it is another of those breads ideal for the beginner; the ratio of effort to success is likely to be good, especially when compared with baguettes although the process is very similar. Concentrate on handling the dough gently and on optimal fermentation and you will have the basis for a perfect sandwich; layer it up with mozzarella, roasted vegetables and herbs and pat yourself on the back while you enjoy it with a glass of something cold in the garden on a summer afternoon.

MAKES 3 LOAVES
600g (1 lb 5 oz) each

Stage 1: Refreshment
16g (½ oz) strong white bread flour
16 g (½ oz) water
8g (¼ oz) wheat starter (8-10 hours after last refreshment)

Stage 2: Refreshment
86g (3¼ oz) strong white bread flour
51g (2 oz) water
21g (¾ oz) caster sugar

Stage 3: Dough mix
578g (1 lb 3 oz) strong white bread flour plus extra for dusting
478g (1 lb ½ oz) water
7g (¼ oz) caster sugar
13g (½ oz) sea salt
sunflower oil, for greasing

1. Place all the stage 1 ingredients in a 500ml (17fl oz) Kilner jar or container with a lid, mix, cover and leave at warm room temperature for 8-12 hours.

2. Add the flour, water and sugar for the stage 2 starter to the jar containing the stage 1 starter, mix, cover and leave at warm room temperature for 6-8 hours.

3. Combine the flour, water, sugar and salt for stage 3 and 170g (6 oz) of starter in a large bowl and mix with a spoon or your hand until no dry patches of flour remain visible. Use one hand rather than two; at this stage the dough is sticky and you are better off keeping one hand free of dough to hold the bowl.

4. Develop the dough in the bowl by hand mixing for 5-8 minutes or, in a free standing mixer fitted with a dough hook, mix for 2-3 minutes on a low speed then 2-3 minutes on a medium speed.

5. Use the sunflower oil to grease a rectangular flat bottomed glass or plastic container with a capacity of at least 2 litres (3½ pints). Transfer the dough to container, cover and rest for 30 minutes.

6. Firmly fold the dough three times, leaving 30 minutes between each fold, then give the dough an additional 30 minutes to rest.

7. Transfer to the fridge, in the container, for 12-36 hours

8. Dust your surface with a thick layer of flour and turn the cold dough out in a single piece onto the floured surface. Sprinkle the top of the dough with more flour. Take a dough cutter or knife and cut the rectangle of dough down the middle starting from a short end to make two long rectangles – the flour on top should stop the blade sticking to the dough. The goal here is to leave the structure of the dough as intact as possible.

9. Line a 25-30cm (10-12 in) long tray or baking dish with a tea towel and dust it with flour. Lift your flour coated pieces of dough, stretching them as little as possible onto the tray or dish. Fold the cloth so it sits between your two loaves.

10. Leave to prove for 1-2 hours at room temperature.

11. Preheat the oven to 240°C/475°F/gas mark 8. Place a baking tray or baking stone in the oven to preheat and place a roasting tin in the bottom of the oven.

12. Carefully lift each ciabatta loaf onto a piece of baking parchment and then transfer on to the preheated oven tray. Pour some water into the preheated tin in the oven, reduce the temperature to 225°C/425°F/gas mark 7, close the door and bake for 15 minutes. Remove the tin of water, and bake for an additional 5-10 minutes until golden brown.

SOURDOUGH CHALLAH

Challah was an important starting point on the journey that led to Margot. When I first began to make it, I wanted better challah than I could buy – made with organic eggs and flour. I started making challah with fresh yeast and experimented until I'd developed a sourdough loaf. Many versions were delicious but lost their shape and barely rose, the difficulty coming with trying to get an enriched dough containing oil to hold a beautiful braid.

The breakthrough came when an Australian baker, Ian Lowe, posted online about his use of sugar in starter to leaven sweet doughs. There were months of trial and error, to be repeated again when the bakery opened but this is the bread I am most proud of; a fermented, delicious bread made with good quality ingredients that I am proud to offer to my family and community for the centre of their Shabbat table.

MAKES 2 LOAVES
700g (1 lb 9 oz) each

Stage 1: Refreshment
30g (1 oz) strong white
bread flour
30g (1 oz) water
15g (½ oz) wheat starter (8–12
hours after last refreshment)

Stage 2: Refreshment
100g (3½ oz) strong white
bread flour
60g (2½ oz) water
25g (1 oz) caster sugar

Stage 3: Dough mix
717g (1 lb 9¼ oz) strong white
bread flour plus extra for
dusting
83g (3¼ oz) whole egg
325g (11½ oz) water,
slightly warm
50g (2 oz) rapeseed oil
67g (2½ oz) Demerara sugar
17g (½ oz) sea salt
rye flour or rice flour,
for dusting
beaten egg, to glaze
20g (¾ oz) sesame seeds

1. Place all the stage 1 starter ingredients in a 1 litre (1¾ pint) Kilner jar or container with a lid, mix, cover and leave at warm room temperature for 8–12 hours.

2. Place the flour, water and sugar for stage 2 plus 50g (2 oz) of the starter in a 1 litre (1¾ pint) Kilner jar or container with a lid, mix, cover and leave at warm room temperature for 8–12 hours.

3. Place the flour, egg, water; rapeseed oil, sugar and salt for stage 3 plus 197g (7 oz) of the starter in a large bowl and mix with a spoon or your hand until no dry patches of flour remain visible. Or, in a free standing mixer fitted with a dough hook, mix for 2 minutes on a low speed to combine ingredients and then 3 minutes on a medium speed. Don't fully develop the gluten at this stage, it will continue to develop with the folds and through the long bulk and shaping process.

4. Develop the dough by hand by kneading it on the work surface, without adding any extra flour, for 5–7 minutes. The dough should be smooth and less sticky after the intial mix.

5. Use the sunflower oil to grease a large mixing bowl or a rectangular flat bottomed glass or plastic container with

a capacity of at least 4 litres (7 pints). Transfer the dough to the bowl or container, cover and rest for 1 hour in a warm place.

6. Fold the dough four times, leaving 1 hour between each fold then give the dough an additional 2 hours to rest. It should turn from a heavy lump of dough into a softer, paler lighter dough with a small increase in volume, around 10–20%.

7. Divide the dough into 12 equal pieces, by weight, and shape into small rounds in the palm of your hand on an unfloured work surface. Flour the top of each piece of dough, the circular motion and traction with the surface tightens up the ball and it will come together in your hand. Try not to get much extra flour into the dough during shaping or the challah will be dry and tough. Pop the dozen balls on a lightly floured surface, cover and leave to rest for 20 minutes. This relaxes the dough so it is easier to roll out the strands to the desired length without them resisting.

8. To roll the strands, shape the dough first. Take a ball of dough, turn it over and flatten it into a rough oval, floured side touching the work surface. Fold one

continued overleaf

longer edge to the middle and then the other edge to meet it in the middle. Then fold the whole piece in half in a rough half circle shape and pinch the seam closed. You should have the beginnings of a fat sausage shaped strand of dough.

9. Using your hands, roll each piece out into a longer strand on a barely floured surface – you need some traction to get the length but it shouldn't stick either. Start from the centre of the strands and roll outwards with even pressure from both hands. You don't want them really long and thin or the challah doesn't get enough height and I am very fond of short, fat braids. Taper the ends with extra pressure as you finish rolling as this helps with the final shape of the braided loaf. Keep all the pieces as uniform in length as possible.

10. Lay 6 strands of dough on a lightly floured surface, meeting at one end. Dust the strands with some rye flour or rice flour to help keep the definition of the braids (also, do practice with wool or string to get better without using uncooperative dough!).

11. To braid a six strand braid is more simple than it appears. It is two repeating movements performed on alternating sides. I use the mantra 'middle, replace' as I braid and can't hold a conversation while braiding or I will lose my place. I have taught bakers at Margot to braid in the way that makes the most sense to them as it varies with the individual. I learned the six strand braid by watching a video online of the wonderful Maggie Glezer demonstrating the technique. To describe with words I will give instructions using numbers and I recommend searching for videos too.

12. You have your six strands in front of you, connected at their tips furthest away from you. Imagine the strands are numbered 1 to 6 left to right. When the strands move position the new strand in the position takes the number so the numbers are 1 to 6, left to right throughout. The centre is always the space between strands 3 and 4.

13. Move strand 6 to the centre and place strand 2 in no. 6 position.
Move strand 1 to the centre and place strand 5 in no. 1 position.

14. Repeat until braid is complete. It always looks like it is going wrong in the middle section; have faith in the process.

15. Add as much tension as you can while braiding, the braid will hold better through the long proof the more tension you can build into it. Pinch the ends and tuck underneath slightly.

16. Line 2 baking trays with baking parchment and place the first completed loaf on a tray. Repeat the braid with the remaining dough to make the second challah and then place on a tray. Leave at room temperature for another 1–3 hours (depending on the time of year and the room temperature) before placing in the fridge, uncovered, for 12–18 hours

17. When the loaves are ready to be baked, preheat the oven to 160ºC/325ºF/ gas mark 3. A gentle heat helps with retaining the shape and avoids it burning on the outside while you wait for the middle to bake.

18. Brush gently with beaten egg and sprinkle with sesame seeds. Bake for 30–35 minutes or until the internal temperature is 98ºC (208ºF) and a skewer inserted into the centre comes out clean. Give it a bit longer if you like a really dark crust. Cool on the trays or a wire rack.

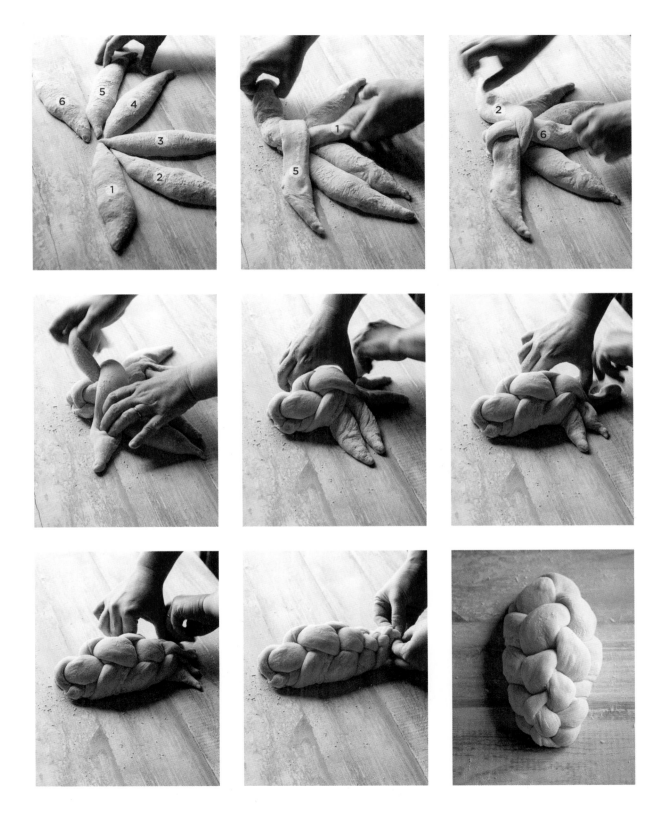

BREAD

LEPESHKA

The year before the bakery opened I was making challah at my synagogue and one of the group was heading off on a trip to Uzbekistan. I had wanted a chekich bread stamp, which are traditionally sold in the market in Bukhara, since reading about them in Gil Marks Encyclopedia of Jewish Food so I asked the gentleman, if he would bring me one back. I had forgotten all about it until over a year later when Roger and Vivienne came by the bakery with bread stamps. That they had remembered and then taken the trouble to find them made me so happy. Sometimes the universe gives us gifts facilitated by kind and generous people if we put the question out there.

Part of my husband's family came from Bukhara, a fascinating Jewish community and I make this bread to maintain the connection for my children with their family history. The loaves for Shabbat, unlike the sweet braided Sabbath bread of European communities were the same as the daily bread only there would be two of them.

MAKES 2 LOAVES
500g (1 lb 2 oz) each

Stage 1: Refreshment
20g (¾ oz) strong white bread flour
20g (¾ oz) water
10g (¼ oz) wheat starter (8–12 hours after last refreshment)

Stage 2: Refreshment
86g (3¼ oz) strong white bread flour
51g (2 oz) water
21g (¾ oz) caster sugar

Stage 3: Dough mix
484g (1lb 1 oz) white bread flour plus extra for dusting
315g (11¼ oz) water
6g (¼ oz) date syrup or caster sugar
15g sunflower oil plus extra for greasing
12g (½ oz) sea salt
clear honey or date syrup, for glazing (optional)
nigella seeds, for sprinkling
dips and salad, to serve

1. Place all the stage 1 ingredients in a 1 litre (1¾ pint) Kilner jar or container with a lid, mix, cover and leave at room temperature for 8–12 hours.

2. Add the stage 2 ingredients to the jar containing the stage 1 starter, mix, cover and leave for 8–10 hours

3. Combine the flour and water for stage 3 in a large bowl and mix with a spoon or your hand until no dry patches of flour remain visible. Or, in a free standing mixer fitted with a dough hook, mix for 2–3 minutes on a low speed. Scrape down the sides, cover and leave for 30–60 minutes.

4. Add 169g (6 oz) of the starter to the bowl with the date syrup or sugar and sunflower oil to the bowl and squeeze the starter through the mix with your hand – use one hand rather than two. Add the salt and squeeze it through the dough.

5. Knead on a flat, unfloured surface by hand for 5–8 minutes. Or, in a free standing mixer fitted with a dough hook, mix for 2 minutes on a low speed and 5 minutes on a medium speed.

6. Use the extra sunflower oil to grease a large mixing bowl or a rectangular flat bottomed glass or plastic container with a capacity of at least 2 litres (3½ pints). Transfer the dough to the bowl or container, cover and rest for 1 hour.

7. Fold the dough twice, leaving 1 hour between each fold, then give the dough an additional 4 hours to rest.

8. Divide the dough in half and shape it into two rounds. Leave to rest on a lightly floured surface uncovered for 20–30 minutes.

9. Take each round of dough and draping it over your knuckles allow the centre of the dough to stretch thinner than the edge. Place onto a lightly floured surface and shape into an even round, approximately 20–23cm (8–9 in) in diameter. Transfer each piece of dough onto a baking parchment.

10. For a crunchy texture bake soon after shaping, for softer, lighter loaves leave to proof for an additional 1–2 hours.

continued overleaf

11. When ready to bake, preheat the oven to 240°C/475°F/gas mark 8. Place 2 baking trays in the oven to heat.

12. Using a bread stamp or fork make patterns in the centre of the bread rounds and around the edges too. Stamping the centre quite thoroughly will allow the outer edges to rise higher than the middle, creating the traditional shape.

13. Glaze with water, mixed with a little honey or date syrup if you like and sprinkle liberally with nigella seeds.

14. Remove the preheated trays from the oven and carefully slide the breads, on the parchment, onto the trays. Bake for 12–18 minutes. Serve warm from the oven with dips and salad. The loaves last for 1–2 days. Store in a bread bin or wrapped in clingfilm or a cloth.

JACHNUN

My friend Clarissa made us the special Yemenite bread, Jachnun for one of the Sheva Brachot meals we had following our wedding. It's a lovely tradition that extends the pleasure of the wedding itself and it allowed us to spend time with family and friends who had travelled from far and wide. Clarissa was taught to make Jachnun by her Yemeni mother in law and they were a revelation to me. These are traditional for Shabbat; the hard work is completed the day before and family gathers together while the oven goes off for 25 hours.

My husband grew up eating baked eggs which are commonly added to slow cooked hot meals prepared for the Sabbath. Our children now also consider 'Shabbas eggs' a particular treat. The eggs develop an intense flavour and the whites turn coffee brown. They can be roasted on a separate tray if you prefer or simmered slowly in a pan of water filled with coffee and onion skins topped with a little oil for half a day.

SERVES 4–6

Stage 1: Refreshment
14g (½ oz) strong white bread flour
14g (½ oz) water
7g (¼ oz) wheat starter (8–12 hours after last refreshment)

Stage 2: Refreshment
67g (2½ oz) strong white bread flour
40g (1½ oz) water
17g (½ oz) caster sugar

Stage 3: Dough mix
740g (1 lb 10 oz) white bread flour
26g (1 oz) caster sugar
370g (13 oz) water
22g (¾ oz) sunflower oil plus extra for greasing
9g (¼ oz) sea salt
200g (7 oz) unsalted butter, melted
2 old slices bread, to line the tin
6 eggs, washed (optional)

To serve
zhoug (a spicy herb paste made with coriander)
6 ripe tomatoes, roughly grated and seasoned with salt

1. Place all the stage 1 ingredients in a 1 litre (1 pint) Kilner jar or container with a lid, mix, cover and leave at room temperature for 8–10 hours.

2. Add the stage 2 ingredients to the jar containing the stage 1 starter, mix, cover and leave for 4–6 hours

3. Combine the flour, sugar, water and oil for stage 3 in a large bowl with 133g (4½ oz) of the starter. Squeeze the starter through the mix with your hand – use one hand rather than two. Add the salt and squeeze it through the dough.

4. Develop the dough in the bowl or knead on a flat, unfloured surface by hand for 5–8 minutes until dough is smooth and no longer sticky or, in a free standing mixer fitted with a dough hook, mix for 2 minutes on a low speed and 5 minutes on a medium speed. The dough should be smooth and start to come away from the sides of the bowl as the gluten develops.

5. Use sunflower oil to grease a large mixing bowl or a rectangular flat bottomed glass or plastic container with a capacity of at least 2 litres (3½ pints). Transfer the dough to the bowl or container, cover and rest for 30 minutes.

6. Divide the dough into 13 x 100g (3½ oz) balls and place on a surface lightly oiled with sunflower oil.

7. Melt the butter and allow to cool a little. Prepare a 25–30cm (10–12 in) baking tin by lining with parchment and the base with the bread – this will absorb any excess butter and will stop the bottom of the pan from burning.

8. Wash the eggs, if using, and cut 6 squares of baking parchment for them to sit on during the long bake.

9. Rub a 30–40cm (12–16 in) section of your work surface and your hands with a little sunflower oil and place a ball of dough in the centre of the oiled section. Squash it with the palm of your hand and working around the edges of the dough begin to stretch it outwards taking care not to tear holes in the dough. If it resists then leave it for a few minutes so the gluten can relax again. As you stretch it 'pin' the edges to the work surface as you work around the dough, it should stretch very thin and you should have a piece of dough roughly 30cm (12 in) square or as big as you can make it without tearing.

continued overleaf

10. Brush the stretched dough lightly with melted butter and fold one third from the right side over the middle third of the dough. Brush the top of the folded piece with melted butter and fold the remaining third over it so you have a vertical rectangle in front of you on the work surface with the shortest side closest to you. Brush the rectangle with melted butter and roll up in a tight cigar from top to bottom. Place in the prepared tin.

11. Repeat with the remaining 12 balls. I often have 2 or 3 pieces on the work surface at a time so I can move between them and they relax a little more while the others are being stretched. Make one layer in the tin and then start a second layer.

12. When they are all rolled and nestled in the tin place the eggs on pieces of paper on top of the dough rolls. If the tin is not very tight fitting, place a piece of foil over the top before putting the lid on.

13. Preheat the oven to 90ºC/200ºF/gas ¼. The oven must not go over 100ºC/225ºF. Cook the bread and eggs for 6–12 hours or overnight. The scent when you wake to these is wonderful. Remove and peel the eggs and serve hot or warm for a leisurely brunch, tear flaky pieces of dough and scoop the zhoug and grated tomato with your fingers.

FLATBREADS

This is a very simple dough, a basic sourdough with very little water. If you roll out some nice even circles of dough with a rolling pin they will pop up like pita bread in the oven. Perfect with dips and simple enough that children or less confident bakers can get involved and get good results as you don't need to deal with sticky dough or shaping here. Vary the seeds depending on what you have in the cupboard or keep it simple with herbs and olive oil or some Parmesan.

MAKES 5 FLATBREADS
200g (7 oz) each

Stage 1: Refreshment
10g (¼ oz) strong white bread flour
10g (¼ oz) water
5g (⅛ oz) wheat starter (8–12 hours after last refreshment)

Stage 2: Refreshment
49g (1¾ oz) strong white bread flour
29g (1 oz) water
12g (½ oz) caster sugar

Stage 3: Dough mix
572g (1¼ lb) strong white bread flour
343g (12 oz) water
10g (¼ oz) sea salt

Toppings
Choose 5 of any of the following:
20–30g (¾–1 oz) nigella seeds, sesame seeds, pumpkin seeds or grated Parmesan
20g (¾ oz) olive oil and a sprinkle of za'atar
20g (¾ oz) olive oil mixed with 10g (¼ oz) date syrup and a pinch of fennel seeds
20g (¾ oz) olive oil and 10g (¼ oz) chopped fresh rosemary and garlic
sunflower oil, for greasing

1. Place all the stage 1 ingredients in a 500ml (17fl oz) Kilner jar or container with a lid, mix, cover and leave at room temperature for 8–12 hours.

2. Add the stage 2 ingredients to the jar containing the stage 1 starter, mix, cover and leave for 4–6 hours

3. Combine the stage 3 ingredients in a bowl with 114g (4 oz) of the starter. Mix with your hand until no dry patches of flour remain visible and a firm dough forms; knead in a bowl or on an unfloured work surface for 5–8 minutes until the dough is smooth and not sticky. Or, in a free standing mixer fitted with a dough hook, mix for 4–5 minutes on a low speed.

4. Use the sunflower oil to grease a large mixing bowl or a rectangular flat bottomed glass or plastic container with a capacity of at least 2 litres (3½ pints). Transfer the dough to the bowl or container, cover and rest for 3–4 hours.

5. The dough can be covered and refrigerated at this stage for up to 24 hours. Remove and allow to come to room temperature for an hour.

6. Divide the dough into 5 x 200g (7oz) pieces and shape into balls. Leave to rest uncovered on a lightly floured surface for 20–30 minutes.

7. Preheat the oven to 240ºC/475ºF/gas mark 8 and place 2 or 3 baking trays in the oven to preheat.

8. With a rolling pin roll the dough into rectangles, the thinner the better but make sure they are evenly rolled or the dough will burn on thinner sections before the rest of the piece is fully baked. Prick with a fork all over to avoid them ballooning in the oven. Brush or spray lightly with water and then add your chosen toppings, using your fingers to lightly press in any seeds or herbs.

9. Place the dough on pieces of baking parchment if you like, to make it easier to transfer into the oven.

10. Place the dough on the preheated trays and bake for 10–12 minutes until golden brown all over and crispy. You may need to bake the breads in batches, depending on the size of the trays.

BREAD

PIZZA DI RECCO

One of our bakers, Daniele, developed the flat dough recipe and told me about this Italian specialty. It took a while to source the Stracchino cheese so we used some blends of cream cheese, mozzarella and Taleggio for the first few we made before discovering that La Fromagerie in Marylebone sells Stracchino. There is no substitute for it really – creamy but with a robust flavour that doesn't fade with baking. I love cheese in and on bread and this is one of my favourite ways to combine the two; simple and incredibly delicious – if you are lucky enough to live near La Fromagerie or another specialty cheese shop then do try it with Stracchino, you won't be disappointed.

MAKES 1 PIZZA
38 x 46cm (15–18 in)

1 x Flatbread dough (complete the recipe on page 57, up until the dough goes into the fridge)
flour, for dusting
600g (1 lb 5 oz) Stracchino cheese or a blend of cheeses including cream cheese, Taleggio and mozzarella
olive oil, for brushing, optional
sunflower oil, for greasing

1. Divide the dough into 2 equal pieces and shape into rounds. Leave to rest, uncovered, on a lightly floured surface for 20–30 minutes.

2. Preheat the oven to 240°C/475°F/gas mark 8. Line a shallow oven tray or roasting tin approximately 38 x 46cm (15–18 in) with baking parchment.

3. Roll out one piece of the dough with a rolling pin, to the size of the tin and using a floured rolling pin to help you move it, transfer it to the tin. Tear the cheese into small pieces and scatter evenly over the dough. Repeat the rolling with the second piece of dough, wet the edges of the piece in the tin and then place the second piece on top. Firmly press all around the edges to seal and cut a few holes in the top of the dough to allow steam to escape. Brush the top with olive oil if you like.

4. Bake for 20–25 minutes until golden brown top and bottom and the cheese is bubbling and hot. Serve hot or warm.

PREPARING PIZZA DI RECCO IN ADVANCE

You can assemble the bread ahead of baking and leave it at this stage for another hour or two, at room temperature, before baking, if preferred.

SOURDOUGH BAGELS

Sourdough bagels are the very best kind of bagel; they are substantial, delicious and don't go rock hard a few hours after being baked. The dough is quite firm and easy to work with so they are a good starting point for sourdough experiments. When the bakery opened, bagels were one of the baked goods most requested by our customers familiar with bagels from North London to New York and we started working on them early on. We keep increasing the numbers we make but it's never enough – they sell out fast especially at weekends.

MAKES 12 BAGELS

Stage 1: Refreshment
17g (½ oz) wheat starter (8–12 hours after its last refreshment)
35g (1¼ oz) water
35g (1¼ oz) strong white bread flour

Stage 2: Refreshment
87g (3¼ oz) water
144g (5 oz) strong white bread flour
36g (1½ oz) caster sugar

Stage 3: Dough mix
530g (1 lb 2½ oz) water
12g (½ oz) malt syrup
450g (1 lb) strong white bread flour
500g (1 lb 2 oz) plain white flour
17g (½ oz) sea salt
sunflower oil, for greasing
rice flour, for dusting

Toppings
For seeded bagels: 300g (11 oz) poppy or sesame seeds.
For Everything bagels: 200g (7 oz) sesame seeds, 100g (3½ oz) nigella seeds,
20g (¾ oz) caraway seeds,
10g (¼ oz) fennel seeds,
2 pinches chilli flakes,
½ tsp sea salt

For baking
malt syrup

1. Place all the stage 1 ingredients in a 500ml (17fl oz) Kilner jar or container with a lid, mix, cover and leave in a warm place for 8–12 hours.

2. Mix the stage 2 starter ingredients into the same jar, cover and leave in a warm place for 8–10 hours.

3. When you are ready to mix the dough, place the water, 303g (11 oz) of starter, malt syrup, flours and salt in a large mixing bowl. Mix with a spoon or your hand until fully combined and then turn out onto a clean work surface and knead for 10 minutes. Do not add any extra flour to the work surface. Use a dough scraper to lift any sticky bits from the surface back into the dough. You can use a free standing mixer fitted with a dough hook if you have one but because the dough is quite dry it may be too much for the machine. If you use a mixer, 10 minutes on a low speed will be sufficient. The dough is ready when is it is no longer sticky and feels smooth and strong.

4. Use the sunflower oil to grease a large mixing bowl or a rectangular flat bottomed glass or plastic container with a capacity of at least 3 litres (5¼ pints). Transfer the dough to the bowl or container, cover and rest for 3 hours in a warm place.

5. Lightly grease a large tray with sunflower oil. Divide the dough into 12 x 150g (5 oz) pieces and roll each into a rough sausage shape. Place in rows, with space between, on the tray, cover with baking parchment or a clean tea towel and allow to rest for 30–40 minutes. This allows the gluten to relax and will give a nice shape to the bagel.

6. Line a large tray with baking parchment and dust the parchment with rice flour. To shape the bagels, take one of the pieces and lay it horizontally in front of you. With both hands together, on the middle of the piece of dough, start rolling with outwards pressure so the pieces extend evenly. You may need to repeat this, starting again from the middle – don't pull the dough to make it longer. When it is about 18–20cm (7–8 in) long, wrap the strand around your four fingers with the join in your palm and roll again on the surface to seal.

7. Lay the bagels on the lined tray and leave at room temperature for 1–2 hours, depending on how warm your kitchen is. Then place in the fridge overnight or for up to 36 hours.

8. When you are ready to bake the bagels, preheat the oven to 220°C/425°F/gas mark 7 and place a roasting tin in oven to preheat. Place the seeds or mixed topping ingredients in bowls. Line 2 baking trays with baking parchment.

9. Pour the water enough water to into a large pan and bring to the boil. Add the malt syrup and then boil the bagels

in batches of 3. Remove from the water after 30 seconds and place on a wire rack to drain. After a minute or two when they are tacky rather than wet (but don't wait too long or they will be too dry to hold the seeds) drop the bagel into the bowl of seeds or mixed topping ingredients and then place on the lined baking tray. Repeat until all the bagels are boiled and coated.

10. Pour water into the preheated tin and place the tray of bagels in the oven and reduce the oven temperature to 200°C/400°F/gas 7. Bake the bagels for 15 minutes then remove tin of water, turn the tray and bake for an additional 10–15 minutes. Leave to cool on the tray.

FREEZING THE BAGELS

Once cooled, the bagels can be frozen. Slice in half before freezing so you can pop them straight in the toaster!

SIMIT

I added these to the baking list after trying a similar bread in a small bakery in Thessaloniki. Simit is the Turkish name for a style of bread widely enjoyed with regional differences and a multitude of names. In Jerusalem street vendors sell a large circular seed-coated bread with a bag of za'atar for dipping, and I recommend it with these too. Ze'ev, a regular visitor to the bakery, brought me some from Israel; a plastic bag filled with vivid green herbs has great potential to be misconstrued when passed over the counter, but the flavour is far superior to the dry dusty versions so often found here in the UK. Look out for it on your travels and ask friends to do the same. Simit are not boiled and are bigger, crunchier and thinner than bagels, but the basic techniques are the same.

MAKES 6 SIMIT

Stage 1: Refreshment
10g (¼ oz) strong white
 bread flour
10g (¼ oz) water
5g (⅛ oz) wheat starter (8–12
hours after last refreshment)

Stage 2: Refreshment
49g (1¾ oz) strong white
bread flour
29g (1 oz) water
11g (¼ oz) caster sugar

Stage 3: Dough mix
353g (12¼ oz) flour
194g (6¾ oz) water
4g (⅛ oz) malt syrup or dark
brown sugar
78g (3 oz) unsalted butter, cut
into pieces
7g (¼ oz) sea salt
sunflower oil, for greasing
200g (7 oz) sesame seeds
rice flour, for dusting

1. Place the stage 1 ingredients in a 500ml (17fl oz) Kilner jar or container with a lid, mix, cover and leave at room temperature for 8–12 hours.

2. Add the stage 2 ingredients to the jar containing the stage 1 starter, mix, cover and leave for 8–10 hours

3. Place the stage 3 flour, water, 113g (4 oz) of the starter, malt syrup or sugar, butter and salt in a large bowl. Mix with a spoon or your hand until fully combined and then turn out onto a clean work surface and knead for 10 minutes. Do not add any extra flour to the work surface. Use a dough scraper to lift any sticky bits from the surface back into the dough. You can use a free standing mixer but because the dough is quite dry it may be too much for the machine. If you use a mixer, mix for 8–10 minutes on a low speed. The dough is ready when is it is no longer sticky and feels smooth and strong.

4. Use the sunflower oil to grease a large mixing bowl or a flat bottomed container with a capacity of at least 1.5 litres (2¾ pints). Transfer the dough to the bowl or container, cover and rest for 3 hours in a warm place.

5. Lightly grease a large tray with sunflower oil. Divide the dough into 6 x 120g (4 oz) pieces and roll into a rough sausage shape. Place on the tray in rows, with space between each one, cover with baking parchment or a clean tea towel and allow to rest for 30–40 minutes to relax the gluten.

6. Place the sesame seeds in a bowl and half-fill a medium bowl with water. Line two baking trays with baking parchment and dust the parchment with rice flour.

7. To shape the simit, take one of the pieces and lay it horizontally in front of you. With both hands together on the middle of the piece of dough, start rolling with outwards pressure so the piece extends evenly. Repeat until it is about 25–30 cm (10–12 in) long (don't pull the dough to make it longer). Connect the ends and roll lightly to seal. Dip the dough briefly the in water and then in the sesame seeds, coating as fully as possible.

8. Lay the simit on the trays, reshape if needed and leave at room temperature for 1–2 hours then place in the fridge overnight or for up to 36 hours.

9. An hour before you are ready to bake the simit, remove them from the fridge. Preheat the oven to 240ºC/475ºF/gas mark 8 and place a roasting tin in oven to preheat. Once it is hot, pour water into the tin, place the simit in oven and reduce the heat to 225ºC/425ºF/gas mark 7. Bake for 10 minutes, remove the water from the oven, reduce the heat to 200ºC/400ºF/ gas mark 6 and bake for a further 5–10 minutes until golden.

BEETROOT BREAD

The extraordinary colour of this dough before baking is a delight. The colour fades to a purplish brown in the heat of the oven but the earthy flavour of the beetroot remains, and the addition of the vegetable purée to the dough makes the crumb soft. The colour of the dough changes during the season for harvesting beetroot, in late summer and early autumn, and it is fascinating to see how it can be so different from one week to the next. Roasting the beetroot preserves the colour and flavour best. This is a regular on the weekend special rotation when beetroot is in season and it is a special that customers ask for often and lament when it passes.

MAKES 1 LOAF
800g (1¾ lb)

Stage 1: Refreshment
70g (2¾ oz) whole wheat bread flour
42g (1½ oz) water
35g (1¼ oz) whole wheat starter (8–12 hours after last refreshment)

For the beetroot purée
300g (11 oz) raw beetroot
53g (2 oz) water

Stage 2: Dough mix
250g (9 oz) white bread flour
62g (2½ oz) whole wheat flour
136g (4½ oz) water
8g (¼ oz) sea salt
rice flour, for dusting
sunflower oil, for greasing

1. Place all stage 1 starter ingredients in a 500ml (17fl oz) Kilner jar or container with a lid, mix, cover and leave at room temperature for 4–6 hours.

2. Preheat the oven to 220ºC/425ºF/gas mark 7. Line a baking tray with baking parchment. Wash, top and tail the beetroot and cut into wedges approximately 5 x 7.5cm (2 x 3 in). Place on the tray, cover with foil and bake for 40 minutes to 1 hour, being careful not to let them burn. The cooked beetroot should be tender and easily pierced with a sharp knife. Allow to cool and then purée with the water in a food processor, until smooth, and set aside.

3 Combine the flours and water for stage 2 with 188g (6½ oz) of the beetroot purée in a large bowl and mix with a spoon or your hand until no dry patches of flour remain visible. Or, in a free standing mixer fitted with a dough hook, mix for 2–3 minutes on a low speed. Scrape down the sides, cover and leave for 30–60 minutes.

4. Add 135g (4½ oz) of the stage 1 starter to the bowl and squeeze it through the mix with your hand – use one hand rather than two; at this stage the dough is sticky and you are better off keeping one hand free of dough to hold the bowl. Add the salt and squeeze it through the dough.

5. Develop the dough in the bowl by hand mixing for 5–10 minutes (see Mixing

the Dough on pages 19–20). Or, in a free standing mixer fitted with a dough hook, mix for another 2 minutes on a low speed and 3–5 minutes on a medium speed.

6. Use the sunflower oil to grease a large mixing bowl or a rectangular flat bottomed glass or plastic container with a capacity of at least 2 litres (3½ pints). Transfer the dough to the bowl or container, cover and rest for 20 minutes.

7. Fold the dough four times, leaving 20 minutes between each fold, then give the dough an additional hour to rest.

8. Pre-shape the dough following the instructions on page 21.

9. Shape the dough into a round loaf following the instructions on pages 21–22.

10. Transfer the dough to a banetton then leave in the fridge for 12–18 hours.

11. Preheat the oven to 240°C/475°F/gas mark 8 for 40 minutes, placing a cast iron pot inside after 20 minutes. Once it is hot, lower the bread into the pot and place the lid on top and return to the oven. Reduce the temperature to 220ºC/425ºF/gas mark 7 and bake for 15 minutes, then reduce the oven temperature again to 200ºC/400ºF/gas mark 6 and bake for a further 15 minutes. Remove the lid and bake for a final 10–15 minutes until it has reached the desired colour.

APPLE, RAISIN AND ROSEMARY BREAD

In Australia 'Raisin toast' is as ubiquitous on café menus and breakfast tables as eggs on toast – it was a staple of my youth in Wollongong alongside coffee, Turkish pide and chicken schnitzel with chips and gravy eaten by the beach. I moved to London and missed easy access to good coffee until within a few years the Antipodeans brought an otherwise perfect city up to speed and began to make good coffee here too.

Rosemary and raisins go so well together; I found this out when I was given Ursula Ferrigno's book *La Dolce Vita* by my friend Siobhan in 2006. Her raisin rosemary bread recipe tucked into the back of a beautiful book of mostly cakes and sweet baking was formative as one of my first successful forays into bread baking.

MAKES 1 LOAF
800g (1¾ lb)

Stage 1: Refreshment
54g (2 oz) strong white
bread flour
32g (1 oz) water
5g (⅛ oz) wheat starter (8–12
hours after last refreshment)

Stage 2: Dough mix
292g (10¼ oz) strong white
bread flour
32g (1 oz) wholegrain rye flour
292g (10¼ oz) water
7g (¼ oz) tsp sea salt
sunflower oil, for greasing
60g (2½ oz) fresh apple, wash
but leave peel on and cut
into rough squares 2cm
(1 in) diameter
60g (2½ oz) raisins
5g (⅛ oz) finely chopped fresh
rosemary
rice flour, for dusting

1. Place all the stage 1 ingredients in a 500ml (17fl oz) Kilner jar or container with a lid, mix, cover and leave at room temperature for 8–12 hours.

2. Combine the flours and water for stage 2 in a large bowl and mix with a spoon or your hand until no dry patches of flour remain visible. Or, in a free standing mixer fitted with a dough hook, mix for 2–3 minutes on a low speed. Scrape down the sides, cover and leave for 30–60 minutes.

3. Add 84g (3¼ oz) of the starter to the bowl and squeeze it through the mix with your hand – use one hand rather than two; at this stage the dough is sticky and you are better off keeping one hand free of dough to hold the bowl. Add the salt and squeeze it through the dough.

4. Develop the dough in the bowl by hand mixing for 5–10 minutes or, in a free standing mixer fitted with a dough hook, mix for 2 minutes on a low speed and 3–5 minutes on a medium speed. This dough has more water than some others, but the raisins will absorb it during the bulk and final proof.

5. Use the sunflower oil to grease a large mixing bowl or a rectangular flat bottomed glass or plastic container with a capacity of at least 2 litres (3½ pints).

6. Transfer the dough to the container, sprinkle the apple, raisins and rosemary on top of the dough, cover and allow to rest for 20 minutes.

7. Fold the dough four times, leaving 20 minutes between each fold, then give the dough an additional hour to rest.

8. Pre-shape the dough following the instructions on page 21.

9. Shape the dough into a batard loaf following the instructions on pages 21–22.

10. Transfer the dough to a banetton then leave in the fridge for 12–18 hours.

11. Preheat the oven to 240°C/475°F/gas mark 8 for 40 minutes, placing a cast iron pot inside after 20 minutes. Once it is hot, lower the bread into the pot and place the lid on top and return to the oven. Reduce the temperature to 220°C/425°F/ gas mark 7 and bake for 15 minutes, then reduce the oven temperature again to 200ºC/400ºF/gas mark 6 and bake for a further 15 minutes. Remove the lid and bake for a final 10–15 minutes until it has reached the desired colour (see the Baking Instructions on page 23).

ROASTED RED PEPPER, GARLIC AND PARMESAN BREAD

Cesar is our head baker and to date the longest serving member of staff at Margot. His father had a bakery in Venezuela while he was growing up and when he develops recipes they often include flavours popular there which prove equally popular with customers in North London. We have a lovely customer, Kata, who travels from Chelsea most weekends with her partner, Miles, and they are always up for trying the weekend specials – this was one of the best ever in her opinion!

MAKES 1 LOAF
800g (1¾ lb)

Stage 1: Refreshment
43g (1½ oz) wholegrain
rye flour
34g (1¼ oz) water
5g (⅛ oz) rye or wheat
starter (8–12 hours after last
refreshment)

Stage 2: Dough mix
356g (12½ oz) strong white
bread flour
305g (11 oz) water
9g (¼ oz) sea salt
sunflower oil, for greasing
rice flour, for dusting

For the flavours
2 medium red peppers,
deseeded and cut into
long strips
olive oil, for drizzling
½ bulb of garlic, cut
horizontally through the middle
30g (1 oz) Parmesan, grated

1. Place all the stage 1 ingredients in a 500ml (17 fl oz) Kilner jar or container with a lid, mix, cover and leave at room temperature for 8–12 hours.

2. Combine the flour and water for stage 2 in a large bowl and mix with a spoon or your hand until no dry patches of flour remain visible. Or, use a free standing mixer fitted with a dough hook and mix for 2–3 minutes on a low speed. Cover and leave for 30–60 minutes.

3. Preheat the oven to 240ºC/475ºF/gas mark 8. Line a baking tray with parchment, place the pepper on the tray and drizzle with olive oil. Place the garlic cut-side down on the tray. Roast for 10–15 minutes until the pepper is soft and has some blackened edges. Allow to cool. When the garlic is cool enough to handle, squeeze the softened cloves from the skin.

4. Add 71g (2¾ oz) of starter to the bowl and squeeze it through the mixture with your hand – use one hand rather than two; at this stage the dough is sticky and you are better off keeping one hand free of dough to hold the bowl. Add the salt and squeeze it through the dough.

5. Develop the dough in the bowl by hand mixing for 5–10 minutes (see Mixing the Dough on pages 19–20). Or, in a free standing mixer fitted with a dough hook, mix for another 2 minutes on a low speed and 3–5 minutes on a medium speed.

6. Use the sunflower oil to grease a large mixing bowl or a rectangular flat bottomed glass or plastic container with a capacity of at least 2 litres (3½ pints). Transfer the dough to the bowl or container, cover and rest for 30 minutes.

7. Spread the roasted red pepper and garlic over the top of the dough. Fold the dough four times, leaving 30 minutes between each fold. Give the dough an additional hour to rest.

8. Pre-shape the dough following the instructions on page 21.

9. Shape the loaf into a batard shape (see the instructions on pages 21–22).

10. Transfer the dough to a banetton then leave in the fridge for 12–18 hours.

11. Preheat the oven to 240°C/475°F/gas mark 8 for 40 minutes, placing a cast iron pot inside after 20 minutes. Score the loaf and then sprinkle with Parmesan. Once the pot is hot, lower the bread into it, place the lid on top and return to the oven. Reduce the heat to 220ºC/425ºF/gas mark 7 and bake for 15 minutes, then reduce the oven temperature again to 200ºC/400ºF/gas mark 6 and bake for a further 15 minutes. Remove the lid and bake for a final 10–15 minutes until it has reached the desired colour (see the Baking Instructions on page 23).

EAST END DATE AND FENNEL BREAD

The East End Sourdough, so called because the bakery is on East End Road which connects East Finchley to Finchley Central, is the base for many of our weekend specials. The leavening comes from the rye starter while the remaining flour in the dough is wheat flour which means the dough can take more water as needed. Dough that contains dried fruit often needs a little more water so the fruit doesn't absorb the water needed to fully hydrate the dough – and it can also hold its structure when other ingredients like cheese are added in. Dates and fennel are amongst those ingredients that divide opinion so I don't put it on the list too often but this is one of my favourite breads. It's wonderful with cheese or with plum jam.

MAKES 1 LOAVES
800g (1¾ lb)

Stage 1: Refreshment
34g (1¼ oz) water
43g (1½ oz) wholegrain rye flour
5g (⅛ oz) rye or wheat starter (8–12 hours after last refreshment)

Stage 2: Dough mix
316g (11¼ oz) strong white bread flour
43g (1½ oz) whole wheat flour
310g (11 oz) water
9g (¼ oz) sea salt
8g (¼ oz) fennel seed, crushed
90g (3¼ oz) roughly chopped, destoned dates (if they are very dry, soak in warm water for an hour and drain)
sunflower oil, for greasing

1. Place all the stage 1 ingredients in a 500ml (17fl oz) Kilner jar or container with a lid, mix, cover and leave at room temperature for 8–12 hours.

2. Combine the flours and water for stage 2 in a large bowl and mix with a spoon or your hand until no dry patches of flour remain visible. Or, in a free standing mixer fitted with a dough hook, mix for 2–3 minutes on a low speed. Scrape down the sides, cover and leave for 30–60 minutes.

3. Add 72g (2¾ oz) of the starter to the bowl and squeeze it through the mixture with your hand – use one hand rather than two; at this stage the dough is sticky and you are better off keeping one hand free of dough to hold the bowl. Add the salt and squeeze it through the dough.

4. Develop the dough in the bowl by hand mixing for 5–10 minutes (see Mixing the Dough on pages 19–20). Alternatively, in a free standing mixer fitted with a dough hook, mix for another 2 minutes on a low speed and 3–5 minutes on a medium speed. Add the fennel seeds and dates to the mix for the last minute or two.

5. Use the sunflower oil to grease a large mixing bowl or a rectangular flat bottomed glass or plastic container with a capacity of at least 2 litres (3½ pints). Transfer the dough to the bowl or container, cover and rest for 30 minutes.

6. Fold the dough four times, leaving 30 minutes between each fold, then give the dough an additional hour to rest.

7. Pre-shape the dough following the instructions on page 21.

8. Shape the dough into a round loaf (see the instructions on pages 21–22).

9. Transfer the dough to a banetton then leave in the fridge for 12–18 hours.

10. Preheat the oven to 240°C/475°F/gas mark 8 for 40 minutes, placing a cast iron pot inside after 20 minutes. Once it is hot, lower the bread into the pot and place the lid on top and return to the oven. Reduce the temperature to 220°C/425°F/gas mark 7 and bake for 15 minutes, then reduce the oven temperature again to 200°C/400°F/gas mark 6 and bake for a further 15 minutes. Remove the lid and bake for a final 10–15 minutes until it has reached the desired colour (see the Baking Instructions on page 23).

CHEDDAR AND PAPRIKA BREAD

I can't now remember exactly where the original spark for the idea for this bread came from – most likely during an absent-minded scroll through Instagram! Paprika is a flavour that I have learned to love only in quite recent years after an Ottolenghi recipe taught me it goes well with cheese. As you may imagine, bakers and bakery staff have as much bread in their homes or on their plates as they require and this is one of the few loaves that everyone at the bakery wants to take home. It may turn bowls, dough tubs and hands red but it really is worth it.

MAKES 1 LOAF
800g (1¾lb)

Stage 1: Refreshment
43g (1½ oz) wholegrain
rye flour
34g (1¼ oz) water
5g (⅛ oz) rye or wheat
starter (8–12 hours after last
refreshment)

Stage 2: Dough mix
321g (11¼ oz) strong white
bread flour
44g (1½ oz) whole wheat flour
315g (11¼ oz) water
9g (¼ oz) sea salt
sunflower oil, for greasing
4g (⅛ oz) extra virgin olive oil
7g (¼ oz) paprika
75g (3 oz) mature Cheddar,
cut into rough 2–3cm
(¾–1¼ in) cubes

1. Place all the stage 1 ingredients in a 500ml (17fl oz) Kilner jar or container with a lid, mix, cover and leave at room temperature for 8–12 hours.

2. Combine the flours and water for stage 2 in a large bowl and mix with a spoon or your hand until no dry patches of flour remain visible. Or, in a free standing mixer fitted with a dough hook, mix for 2–3 minutes on a low speed. Scrape down the sides, cover and leave for 30–60 minutes.

3. Add 73g (2¾ oz) of the starter to the flour and water mix and squeeze the starter through the mix with your hand – use one hand rather than two; at this stage the dough is sticky and you are better off keeping one hand free of dough to hold the bowl. Add the salt and squeeze it through the dough.

4. Develop the dough in the bowl by hand mixing for 5–10 minutes (see Mixing the Dough on pages 19–20). Or, in a free standing mixer fitted with dough hook, mix for another 2 minutes on a low speed and 3–5 minutes on a medium speed.

5. Use the sunflower oil to grease a large mixing bowl or a rectangular flat bottomed glass or plastic container with a capacity of at least 2 litres (3 pints). Transfer the dough to the bowl or container, cover and rest for 30 minutes.

6. Combine the olive oil and paprika in a small bowl. Spread the red paste over the top of the dough in the container with your hand or a spoon and then sprinkle the Cheddar evenly on top. Adding the paprika before the folds gives a swirled effect to the dough.

7. Fold the dough four times, leaving 30 minutes between each fold, then give the dough an additional hour to rest.

8. Pre-shape the dough following the instructions on page 21.

9. Shape the dough into a batard loaf following the instructions on pages 21–22.

10. Transfer the dough to a banetton then leave in the fridge for 12–18 hours.

11. Preheat the oven to 240°C/475°F/gas mark 8 for 40 minutes, placing a cast iron pot inside after 20 minutes. Once it is hot, lower the bread into the pot and place the lid on top and return to the oven. Reduce the temperature to 220°C/425°F/gas mark 7 and bake for 15 minutes, then reduce the oven temperature again to 200°C/400°F/gas mark 6 and bake for a further 15 minutes. Remove the lid and bake for a final 10–15 minutes until it has reached the desired colour (see the Baking Instructions on page 23).

DOLOMITE RYE, WALNUT AND RAISIN LOAF

The Dolomite rye is another of our baker Daniele's contributions to Margot, inspired by his travels in the region not too far from his home in Northern Italy. The German influences on the bread of the Dolomites is pronounced compared to other breads that I more readily associate with Italian baking. Rye is grown in the region and is used in breads designed to keep well; for months at a time in some cases. Some of our customers prefer it without the caraway and you can leave it out but even with only rye, raisins and walnuts it is a complex and interesting bread. Slice thinly and wrap it well and it should keep you going for a while, if not quite through the winter.

MAKES 1 LOAF
1kg (2 lb)

Stage 1: Refreshment
37g (1½ oz) wholegrain
rye flour
30g (1 oz) water
5g (⅛ oz) rye starter (8–10
hours after last refreshment)

For the toasted walnuts
75g (3 oz) walnuts

Soaker
64g (2½ oz) raisins
64g (2½ oz) water
11g (¼ oz) caraway seeds
(optional)

Stage 2: Dough mix
428g (15 oz) wholegrain
rye flour
321g (11¼ oz) water
11g (¼ oz) sea salt
rice flour, for dusting
sunflower oil, for greasing

1. Place all the stage 1 ingredients in a 200ml (7 fl oz) Kilner jar or container with a lid, mix, cover and leave at room temperature for 8–10 hours.

2. At the same time as the starter is prepared, combine the seeds and cold water for in a 200ml (7 fl oz) container. Cover and leave at room temperature.

3. Preheat the oven to 180ºC/350ºF/gas mark 4. When the oven is hot, place the walnuts on a baking tray and toast for 5–10 minutes until fragrant.

4. Combine the flour, water and salt for stage 2 in a bowl. Add 64g (2½ oz) of the starter, the toasted walnuts and soaker ingredient and mix with a spoon or your hand until no dry patches of flour remain visible. Or, in a free standing mixer fitted with a dough hook, mix for 2–3 minutes on a low speed.

5. Place the rice flour in a large bowl. Line a baking tray with baking parchment.

5. Shape the dough into a round with wet hands on the work surface – the internal shaping process is not needed here as there is little gluten to work with. Toss the dough in the rice flour and place seam-side down on the lined tray. You can allow the bread to proof for 3–4 hours at room temperature before baking or proof in the fridge for 16–20 hours and bake from cold the following day.

6. Preheat the oven to 240ºC/475ºF/gas mark 8 for 20 minutes and place a cast iron pot inside to preheat for another 20 minutes.

7. Cut around the piece of parchment the loaf has been proofed on leaving strips on either side of the loaf to help you transfer it into the pot. Don't score this loaf, there is relatively little oven spring and the dough should crack open during baking leaving sections of the dough showing between patches of rice flour.

8. Lower the bread into the pot, replace the lid and return to the oven. Reduce the temperature to 220ºC/425ºF/gas mark 7 and bake for 15 minutes, then reduce the oven temperature again to 200ºC/400ºF/gas mark 6 and bake for a further 15 minutes. Transfer the loaf to a baking tray and bake for another 20–30 minutes until the internal temperature is 100ºC and a skewer inserted into the centre comes out clean.(see the Baking Instructions on page 23).

9. Allow to cool completely on a wire rack and don't slice the loaf for at least 12 hours after baking.

SOURDOUGH
PASTRY

SOURDOUGH LAMINATED PASTRY DOUGH

This is the dough that we use to make all our pastries – from favourites such as pain aux raisins and croissants to our not so traditional rugelach and savoury cheese twists. The trimmings created during the lamination stage can be used to make a simple, light brioche loaf which is good on its own and which we use to make Bostock. The process of building perfect layers of butter between layers of dough is time consuming but is almost magical; the process, even when you do it day in and day out, remains satisfying in its precision and rhythm.

MAKES 1.35KG (3 LB) DOUGH
1–1.25kg (2¼–2¾ lb)

Ready in 4 days

Stage 1: Refreshment
25g (1 oz) strong white bread flour
25g (1 oz) water
13g (½ oz) wheat starter (8–12 hours after last refreshment)

Stage 2: Refreshment
112g (4 oz) white bread flour
67g (2½ oz) water
28g (1 oz) caster sugar

Stage 3 Dough mix
525g (1 lb 2½ oz) white bread flour plus extra for dusting
152g (5¼ oz) water
63g (2½ oz)/1½ whole eggs, beaten
105g (3¾ oz) sugar
11g (¼ oz) sea salt
350g (12 oz) unsalted butter, chilled

MAKING THE DOUGH

1. Place all the stage 1 ingredients in a 1 litre (1¾ pint) jar or container with a lid, mix, cover and leave at warm room temperature for 10–14 hours.

2. Add the flour, water and sugar for the stage 2 starter to the jar containing the stage 1 starter, mix, cover and leave at warm room temperature for 12–16 hours.

3. Place the flour, water, eggs, sugar, salt and 236g (8¼ oz) of the starter in a free standing mixer fitted with a dough hook. Mix for 5 minutes on low speed. Scrape down the sides, mix on medium speed for 10–12 minutes.

4. Roughly shape the dough into a 10 x 15cm (4 x 6 in) rectangle and wrap in clingfilm. Set aside in a warm place for 3 hours. Ideally the room temperature should be 24ºC (75ºF) or more – if the temperature is less than this place a tray of warm water in the oven (not turned on) and place the dough inside. In summer room temperature will usually be fine.

5. Transfer the dough to the fridge for 2–3 hours.

PREPARING THE BUTTER

1. Meanwhile, take the butter out of the fridge and allow to sit at room temperature for 30–60 minutes, depending on the room temperature. In summer you may not need to leave it out at all. The butter needs to be in a block – you can use two pieces pushed together.

2. Place the pieces of butter between two sheets of baking parchment and hit it firmly with a rolling pin, starting from one side and moving along the piece of butter, then turning it and repeating the process. Keep turning and hitting it until you have a rectangle roughly 15 x 20cm (6 x 8 in), 5–8mm (¼–⅜ in) thick. Finish by rolling with the rolling pin a little to make sure it is even. If you end up with a slightly irregular shape, reshape into a more perfect rectangle by cutting bigger edges from the rectangle with a small sharp knife and placing them where the edges are shorter, pushing the pieces together like a jigsaw puzzle. The butter should still be fairly cold when you finish shaping it and pliable, like firm rubber.

3. Wrap the dough and put it back in the fridge. Remove 30–60 minutes before it is time to laminate the dough. Again, this may not be necessary in warmer months. The goal is to have the butter pliable though neither melting nor rock hard; the dough and butter should have a similar texture when the lamination begins.

LAMINATION

1. Peel the parchment paper off the butter and dust one side generously with flour. Turn it over and do the same with the other side. Set aside

2. Lightly flour the work surface. Lay the dough on the work surface with one of the longest sides closest to you and lightly dust with flour. Working from the centre out, begin to roll into a 30 x 20cm (12 x 8 in) rectangle.

3. Place the butter in the centre of the dough with the shortest side of the butter closest to you. Lift the two sides of the dough so they meet in the middle, completely covering the butter. Pinch the seam where the dough meets over the butter with your fingers to seal it. The open ends where the butter is visible will be the shorter ends at the top and bottom of the rectangle in front of you.

4. Make a long cut from top to bottom with a sharp knife down the length of each of the closed sides of the dough, where it has been folded. It should be quite deep but not quite deep enough to reach the butter.

5. Turn the dough so the two open ends are now facing outwards. One long, cut-side will be closest to you.

6. Begin to roll outwards again, using even pressure, starting from the centre of the rectangle. Make sure your dough has just enough flour so the dough does not stick to the work surface or rolling pin. Try not to push so firmly that the butter comes out of the open ends

7. When the dough is 50–60cm (20–24 in) on the longest side, trim the open outer edges of the rectangle with a sharp knife. Trim where the butter ends

to keep maximum butter in the laminated dough. If you are not sure then trim a little and look at the dough you have cut. If there is some butter sandwiched between dough then no need to cut further. The cuts don't need to be perfectly straight; you can manipulate the dough so they meet when you fold it again.

8. Take the two short ends and fold them onto the centre of the dough one at a time. They should meet approximately one third from the left end. Gently push the edges together keeping the enclosed single layer of butter hidden.

9. Take the right side of your folded dough and fold over the left side, folding exactly in half. As before, make a cut in the outer edges of the dough. On the right side you will cut through a single edge of dough (the spine, where the dough was folded) and on the left side there will be two edges one on top of the other. Make a cut in both. The cutting allows the butter to extend as fully as possible to the edges of the dough, reducing wastage.

10. Wrap the dough in clingfilm and place in the fridge to rest for 45–60 minutes.

11. Remove the dough from the fridge and place on the work surface. Turn it so a longer, cut-side is closest to you. Begin to roll again as before, left and right, to form a rectangle, 50–60cm (20–24 in).

12. Trim the short edges again cautiously. You will see four layers inside the full length of each short side, repeat the folding as before. Fold the outer edges to meet one third from the left of your long rectangle, and then fold in half from the right.

13. Wrap in clingfilm and place back in the fridge for 12–20 hours or overnight.

FINAL ROLL FOR CROISSANTS OR PAIN AU CHOCOLAT

1. Remove the dough from the fridge. If it is very firm and cold, leave it for 20–30 minutes before rolling.

2. The short sides need to be around 30–32cm (12–12¾ in) long. If they are not, then roll the dough to lengthen them until they reach this measurement. Lay the rectangle on a lightly dusted work surface with one longest side closest to you and the short sides facing outwards. Begin to roll with firm movements from the centre of the rectangle outwards towards the short sides. Roll until the dough is 3–5mm (⅛–¼ in) thick. If it is resisting too much then wait 5–10 minutes to allow the gluten to relax before continuing.

3. When you have your long rectangle of dough, trim a small amount off the full length of the long side closest to you, very close to the edge in as straight a line as you can manage. This exposes the lamination inside so when the croissants are shaped, they can expand fully.

4. Use this line to measure an exact distance from the cut edge to the top of the rectangle, marking your measurement with small knife cuts. The dough won't likely be the same length along the full length so choose an appropriate measurement around the 28–32cm (11–12¾ in) mark. For example if the left side is measuring 30cm (12 in) from the cut-side to the top, in the middle it is 32cm (12¾ in) and at the right end it is 30.5cm (12¼ in) you will measure at 30cm (12 in). Cut from mark to mark so your rectangle is exactly 30cm (12 in) high from top to bottom across its full length. Ignore the rounded and tapered ends of the rectangle as they will be trimmed off; it is the main section of the dough you need to worry about at this stage. On the far left short side, using a ruler, trim the edge of the dough where it begins to taper.

FINAL PROOFING THE PASTRIES

1. Place the pastries on baking trays lined with parcement, about 5–7.5cm (2–3 in) apart as they will increase significantly in volume during proofing.

2. At this stage the pastries can be chilled in the fridge for 24–36 hours before proofing and baking. Otherwise begin the final 20–24 hour proof immediately. We proof the pastries at 24ºC (75ºF) in our purpose-built cabinet. To recreate this at home put them in an enclosed space with some warm water, the oven for example, or build a frame with plastic or clingfilm and put somewhere warm. On a warm humid day, leaving at room temperature may be enough. Without some warmth for this final proof they may not do very much at all.

3. When the pastries are ready to bake they should look light and puffy and have increased in volume by 30–40%. If you are not sure they are ready, bake half and see how they come out. Then you can still give the other half further proofing time before baking if needed.

GLAZING AND BAKING THE PASTRIES

1. Preheat the oven to 200ºC/400ºF/gas mark 6.

2. If glazing, brush the pastries with egg beaten with a pinch of salt. Try not to get much egg on the cut laminated sides.

3. Place in the oven, add steam (see page 23) and immediately reduce the temperature to 180ºC/350ºF/gas mark 4. Bake for 15 minutes then remove the steam tin and turn the baking trays around. Bake for another 10–15 minutes, until the pastry is a deep golden colour, tinged brown at the edges.

WHY AREN'T THEY PERFECT

If the pastries are leaking butter then it may indicate under-proofing or imperfect lamination, but they will still be edible and delicious. Cut one and have a look at the inside – if the texture is cakey then the butter may have been too warm during lamination and the layers are indistinct. If they are too dry, increase the water a little in the mix or try a different, softer flour. If they collapse and are flat they were probably over proofed.

There are always a few misshapen and imperfect ones in any batch – these are ideal for Twice Baked Croissants (see page 102–3) so be glad indeed.

CROISSANTS

I often travelled to Paris when we used to visit my husband's grandmother. The loyalty to the croissants of one bakery or another surprised me. Baguettes might be bought from one boulangerie but croissants from another. In the UK we have borrowed the format of the pastry and its familiarity is embedded but we have not yet, for the most part, adopted the care with which they are made or appreciation for a truly special croissant. We have never sold a premade, baked-from-frozen croissant at Margot and will never do so and I hope with time we see more handmade pastries, including sourdough pastries, available in more bakeries and cafes here too.

MAKES 10 PASTRIES

1 x quantity Sourdough Laminated Pastry Dough (see pages 80–82 including the final roll stage)
beaten egg, to glaze
pinch of salt

1. With a ruler and a small sharp knife, mark 3 small indents on the rectangle of pastry, 8cm (3¼ in) apart starting from the left bottom corner and marking along the bottom edge of the rectangle. Mark the top of the rectangle of dough vertical to your first small cut at the bottom. Measure and mark 1 indent 4cm (1½ in) to the left of your mark at the top left corner of your rectangle and from this mark, measure 3 indents, 8cm (3¼ in) apart, along the top of your rectangle of dough.

2. Use a ruler and a small sharp knife to cut neat lines, indent to indent, making triangles. The first triangle will be too small; put it aside. Each triangle will then be 8cm long at its base, the tip of one is the beginning of the base of the next and the triangles alternate along the dough, one right way up and one upside down. Weigh the second or third of your triangles and if it is 90–120g (3¼–4 oz) continue with the 8cm (3¼ in) size for the base of your triangles. We usually check the weight of the cut triangles at the beginning and again in the middle of cutting a block to ensure consistency. If your dough weighs a lot less or a lot more than this then adjust your measurement – go down if your croissant triangle weighs more than 120g (3¾ oz) and go up to 8.5-9cm (3⅜–3½ in) if it weighs too little, cut a fewl more and check the weight again.

3. Work quickly left to right, cutting all your dough into triangles. When you reach the far right tapered end and can no longer cut croissants then stop. Reserve the end pieces to make Rugelach (see page 91) or if they are big enough they can be used for some of the other recipes in the section that don't require perfect lamination such as the Blue Cheese and Red Onion Marmalade twists (see page 96) or Pumpkin and Provolone Roll (see page 99). Put them back in the fridge until you are ready to use them.

4. To roll the croissants, have the base of the triangle closest to you. Begin the roll with your fingers but not too tightly – try and leave a hollow gap as the roll begins. Start with your fingertips and then with the palm of your hand roll in a firm, straight movement away from your body so the croissant shape forms as it rolls over itself. The pointy end should be underneath the croissant when you set it down on the baking tray.

5. Follow instructions for Final Proofing the Pastries and Glazing and Baking the Pastries on page 82. Cool the croissants on the tray.

SOURDOUGH PASTRY

PAIN AU CHOCOLAT

We use Valrhona chocolate beans cut in half because the quality and flavour is excellent compared to some overly sweet bars that can be bought for commercial pain au chocolat production. I suggest you do as we do in choosing your chocolate when making these and use the chocolate you best like to eat. It melts inside the pastries anyway so a rough line of chopped chocolate pieces is absolutely fine. The couple of times we used made-for-purpose batons for pain au chocolat I was disappointed. If you are going to spend days making chocolate-filled pastries then the chocolate should be excellent.

MAKES 10 PASTRIES

1 x quantity Sourdough Laminated Pastry Dough (see pages 80–82 including the final roll stage)
200g (7 oz) good quality chocolate cut into rough, chunky pieces
beaten egg, to glaze
pinch of salt

1. Measure and trim the top and bottom of the rectangle as for the Croissants (see page 84), trim the dough by cutting a vertical line where the lamination is complete on the far left end of the dough. You are going to cut the dough into two, long thin rectangles by dividing it in half along the middle horizontally so measure the halfway point and make 3 or more marks and then cut the dough in half using the marks as a guide.

2. Make three, 8cm (3¼ in) indents along the top and bottom of the rectangle starting from the top left and bottom left corners. Cut vertical lines from indent to indent and weigh one small rectangle which should be between 90g–120g (3¼–4 oz). If it is then continue to mark and cut until you have 10–12 small rectangles, approximately 8 x 15cm (3¼–6 in) with the short sides closest to you.

3. Lay your chocolate in two lines on each small rectangle following the bottom of the rectangle. Lay one line 1–2cm (½–¾ in) from the bottom and the next line 2–3cm (¾–1¼) in above that. When all the chocolate is in place, start to roll the bottom edge over your first line of chocolate and then, with a firm movement starting from fingertips to the palm of your hand, roll to the end of the rectangle. The seam won't be tucked under but should be close to the tray when you place your pastry in position for proofing.

4. Follow instructions for Final Proofing the Pastries and Glazing and Baking the Pastries on page 82.

PAIN AUX RAISINS

These are fat and tall when shaped, so don't be confused by their dissimilarity to the more familiar shape of the baked pastry. They collapse as they proof and bake, spreading outwards; allow plenty of space between them on the tray. Bake to a bold golden brown: the contrast of the fully baked pastry with the soft, custard-filled and syrup-soaked interior is wonderful.

MAKES 10 PASTRIES

1 x quantity Sourdough Laminated Pastry Dough (see pages 80-81)
300g (11 oz) Crème Pâtissèrie (see page 202)
200g (7 oz) raisins
200g (7 oz) Simple Syrup (see page 205)

1. To shape the pain aux raisins, measure and trim all 4 edges of the pastry rectangle. Using a palette knife or spatula spread the crème pâtissière over the pastry, in an even layer, leaving a 1–2cm (½–¾ in) border at the top of the rectangle. Sprinkle the raisins over the crème pâtissière.

2. Roll up the dough, from the bottom long edge to the top, with some tension as you roll. Pinch the seam firmly to close it and then arrange your roll so the seam side is down, touching the work surface.

3. With a ruler, measure your roll and divide the final length by 10. Each piece should be approximately 5–6cm (2–2½ in). Mark indents and then cut with a sharp knife.

4. Place the pastries cut-side down on the baking trays and proof for 20–24 hours following the instructions for Final Proofing the Pastries on page 82. Pain aux raisins do not need to be glazed before baking; once proofed follow instructions for Baking the Pastries on page 82.

5. After baking, as soon as they come out of the oven, brush the pastries generously with the syrup.

RUGELACH

This ever popular Jewish pastry can be made with a whole quantity of dough or using leftover trimmings from other pastries. I have still never eaten a rugelach baked anywhere but Margot, though have often carefully examined images of the rugelach of the bakeries of Tel Aviv and New York. Leavening rugelach with sourdough makes the pastries less than traditional, and possibly completely unique to Margot, but the shape and filling is familiar. They are small and are deceptively delicious. My youngest son considers these the best of the Margot products and will proudly tell all the customers in the queue to buy them when he gets the chance.

MAKES 48 PASTRIES

1 x quantity Sourdough Laminated Pastry Dough (see pages 80-81)
1 x quantity of Chocolate filling or 1 x quantity of Tahini and Date Filling (see below)
1 x quantity of Simple Syrup (see page 205)

1. The dough for rugelach should be rolled thinner than for other pastries – roll it out as thin as you can, ideally to 3mm (⅛ in) thickness.

2. Cut out 3 x 25cm (10 in) circles with a sharp knife (use a cake tin or a plate as a template), they don't have to be perfectly round.

3. Use a palette knife or a spatula to spread 50g (2 oz) of your chosen filling onto each circle, leaving a 1cm (½ in) border, without filling, around the outer edge of the circle.

4. Cut the circles into quarters with a small sharp knife, like cutting a pizza. Divide each quarter into 4 triangles so you have 16 triangles in total. They don't all need to be exactly the same size.

5. From the outer edge, roll a triangle towards the middle of the circle. Repeat until all the triangles have been rolled up. Arrange in lines on a tray, close together.

6. Follow instructions for Final Proofing the Pastries on page 82. Rugelach do not need to be glazed before baking; once proofed follow instructions for Baking the Pastries on page 82.

7. After baking, as soon as they come out of the oven, brush the pastries generously with the syrup.

FILLINGS

CHOCOLATE FILLING

In a medium heatproof bowl place 15g (½ oz) cocoa powder, 70g (3 oz) chopped dark chocolate and 20g (¾ oz) date syrup. Heat 60g (2½ oz) butter until melted and bubbling and pour over the chocolate mixture. Stand for 5 minutes and then stir. Some lumps may remain but it doesn't matter. Cool for 30 minutes before using.

TAHINI AND DATE FILLING

In a medium bowl place 75g (3 oz) tahini and 75g (3 oz) date syrup. Stir well to combine. Sprinkle with 75g (3 oz) toasted sesame at the end of the final proof.

SOURDOUGH PASTRY

DANISH PASTRIES

Danish pastries come in many shapes but ours are designed to best contain the filling after their long final proof; the well formed in the centre is able to hold custard and fruit perfectly. They are pretty with their bright fruits and provide colour and contrast on a counter so full of shades of brown. We like to vary the fruit we use in our Danish pastries, according to what's in season. We use rhubarb for as long as it is pink and summer fruits for as long as we have them; apricot or plum Danish when they are at their best are truly special. Each of the quantities of fruit below will fill eight pastries. You can just one fruit filling or try a mixture.

MAKES 8 PASTRIES

1 x quantity Sourdough Laminated Pastry Dough (see pages 80–81)
beaten egg, to glaze
pinch of salt
1 x quantity Crème Pâtissière (see page 202)
1 x quantity Simple Syrup (see page 205)
icing sugar, for dusting

For the fruit fillings
160g (5½ oz) blueberries, blackberries or raspberries
4 apricots, halved
4 peaches, cut into thin slices
4 apples, cut into thin slices
4 small poached pears, halved
24 x 3cm (1¼ in) pieces of pink rhubarb (sprinkled with half their weight in sugar and baked at 200°C/400 F°C/gas mark 6 for 15 minutes)

1. After the bottom of the pastry rectangle is measured and trimmed (see page 82), cut a vertical line down where the lamination is complete on the far left end of the dough. Do not trim the top edge yet.

2. Measure and make three sets of indents 9cm (3½ in) apart on the left short end of your rectangle. Make another set in the centre of the rectangle and another set towards the far right end. This will mark where you will divide the short side of the rectangle into 3 with the top of edge of the rectangle remaining untrimmed for the moment. Then cut straight lines, using a ruler, along the horizontal, longer length of the rectangle. Discard any excess trimmed at the top of the dough.

3. Make 9cm (3½ in) indents along the top and bottom of the rectangle and cut vertical lines from indent to indent, dividing all the dough into 9cm (3½ in) squares. Use the cutter to remove a circle from of the centre of half of your squares.
4. Brush the edges of the squares without

the circle cut out lightly with water and lay a square with the cut out on top so you have two layers of laminated dough and a 'well' in the centre – you can use other shapes too, just try to keep a 2cm (¾ in) edge from the cut section to outer edge so they don't collapse and lose their filling when baked.

5. Follow instructions for Final Proofing the Pastries on page 82.

6. Follow instructions for Glazing and Baking the Pastries on page 82 but before baking, pipe or spoon approximately 40g (1½ oz) crème pâtissière into each pastry and top with fruit.

7. After baking, brush the pastries with the syrup and when cool, dust with icing sugar.

BLUE CHEESE AND RED ONION MARMALADE TWISTS

Savoury pastries always sell well in the bakery; I think we are collectively able to convince ourselves that a savoury pastry is permissible while a sweet one is a treat. The combination of sweet marmalade and salty cheese is stunning here; they also work with other cheeses such as grated Parmesan or Cheddar and you can omit the marmalade or use a good shop bought one if you don't have time to make the version on page 212.

MAKES 10 PASTRIES

1 x quantity Sourdough Laminated Pastry Dough (pages 80–81)
300g (11 oz) soft, spreadable blue cheese or 150g (5 oz) blue cheese mixed with 150g (5 oz) cream cheese
200g (7 oz) Red Onion Marmalade (see page 212)

1. Trim all 4 edges of the pastry dough rectangle. Measure and mark the rectangle into thirds along the bottom edge. Spread the two thirds of the dough to the far right of the rectangle with blue cheese and then the marmalade in even layers, right to the edges. Leave the third at the far left without topping.

2. Fold the third with no topping onto the middle third of the dough. And fold the third of the dough at the far right with topping onto the left third.

3. Turn the rectangle so the closed end is furthest away from you. Measure the dough along the bottom edge and divide length in centimetres by 10. Cut the rectangle vertically into 10 even-sized strips with a sharp knife.

4. Cut each strip in half, down its longest length leaving 2cm (¾ in) attached at the top.

5. Twist the two 'legs' of your piece around each other in a simple braid; they can be a bit messy but don't worry.

6. Follow instructions for Final Proofing the Pastries on page 82. The twists do not need to be glazed before baking – once proofed follow instructions for Baking the Pastries on page 82.

SOURDOUGH PASTRY

PUMPKIN AND PROVOLONE ROLLS

These came about when we were making a pumpkin sourdough bread and had extra pumpkin to use up. If Provolone is difficult to find use Mozzarella and Parmesan instead. Any firmish filling that works in a galette or tart will work well inside the slightly sweet laminated pastry; just make sure it is properly seasoned. Taleggio or blue cheese both work well instead of the provolone. Or use feta cheese with dried chilli flakes and fresh oregano leaves instead of the sage. You can piece together trimmings after shaping other pastries to make a smaller version of this roll too; perfect lamination is not so important here.

MAKES 2 PASTRIES

1 medium pumpkin or butternut squash, approximately 1.5kg (3 lb 6 oz), peeled, deseeded and chopped into 4–5cm (1½–2 in) pieces
1 small bunch of sage
50g (2 oz) olive oil
500g (1 lb 2 oz) provolone cheese, roughly cubed or crumbled
1 x quantity Sourdough Laminated Pastry Dough (pages 80–81)
beaten egg, to glaze
salt and freshly ground black pepper

1. Preheat the oven to 220ºC/425ºF/gas mark 7. Line a baking tray with baking parchment.

2 Place the pumpkin or squash pieces on the lined tray, drizzle the olive oil over and season with salt. Roast for 30–40 minutes until tender and caramelised at the edges. Chop the sage leaves and add for the last 5 minutes. Set aside to cool.

3. Gently combine 1kg (2¼ lb) of the cooled roasted pumpkin or squash in a bowl with the cheese. Season generously – it should be well seasoned as the pastry is slightly sweet and not very salty.

4. Roll out the pastry dough and trim all 4 edges of your rectangle. Cut the rectangle of dough in half vertically down the middle. Arrange half the filling in a long mound, on one piece of pastry, 5cm (2 in) or so from the bottom of the dough and not quite reaching the sides. Lift the bottom edge, closest to you, up and over the filling and then roll the dough fully so the filling is encased in the pastry. Pinch the seam closed and close the ends by pushing down on them with the side of your hand. Repeat with the remaining dough and filling to make another roll. Transfer the rolls to a baking tray, side by side but with a 13cm (5 in) gap between as they will expand during proofing and baking. Cut some diagonal lines along the top of each roll so steam can escape when it is baking.

5. Proof the rolls for 20–24 hours until they look light and fluffy, following the instructions for Final Proofing the Pastries on page 82.

6. After proofing, glaze with egg wash and bake for 30–40 minutes until golden brown and piping hot in the centre. Serve hot, warm or cold.

TWICE BAKED CROISSANTS

The only way to make a sourdough croissant or pain au chocolat more delicious is to fill it and bake it again. We like to be creative with these so besides the ever present and much-loved almond croissants, which we have daily, variations on twice baked croissants appear on weekends as specials and each flavour runs for a month or so at a time. It's an old bakery trick to make twice baked croissants – they give new life to leftover pastries that would otherwise be thrown away in a similar vein to making bread and butter pudding or treacle tart to use up leftover bread. Any baker or pastry chef who has committed time to the process of laminating, proofing and baking croissants can't bear to see them wasted.

TWICE BAKED ALMOND CROISSANTS

MAKES 6 PASTRIES

6 x 1–2 day old pastries
1 x quantity of Simple Syrup (see page 205)
1 x quantity of Almond Frangipane (see page 203)
30g (1 oz) flaked almonds
icing sugar, for dusting

1. Preheat the oven to 180ºC/350ºF/gas mark 4. Line a baking tray with baking parchment.

2. Slice the croissants through the centre, horizontally, so the pastry opens up like a sandwich. Dip the cut-side of both halves in the syrup and place cut-side up on the lined tray. Place 30g (1 oz) frangipane inside and 20g (¾ oz) frangipane on top of each croissant. Sprinkle with flaked almonds.

3. Bake the croissants for 15 minutes, turn the tray and bake for an additional 10–15 minutes. They should be lightly caramelised underneath and golden on top but not too dark. Allow to cool a little and dust with icing sugar before serving.

TWICE BAKED HAZELNUT AND CHOCOLATE CROISSANTS

MAKES 6 PASTRIES

6 x 1–2 day old pastries
1 x quantity of Simple Syrup (see page 205)
1 x quantity of Hazelnut Chocolate Frangipane (see page 203)
150g (5 oz) 64% dark chocolate, roughly broken
cocoa powder, for dusting

1. Pre-heat the oven to 180ºC/350ºF/gas mark 4. Line a baking tray with parchment.

2. Slice the croissants through the centre, horizontally, so the pastry opens up like a sandwich. Dip the cut-side of both halves in the syrup and place cut-side up on the lined tray. Place 50g (2 oz) chocolate hazelnut frangipane inside each croissant.

3. Bake the croissants for 15 minutes, turn the tray and bake for an additional 10–15 minutes. They should be lightly caramelised underneath and golden on top but not too dark. Allow to cool a little.

4. Place the chocolate in a heatproof bowl and place over a pan of gently simmering water. Stir occasionally until melted.

5. Dip one half of the top of each croissant in the melted chocolate. Dust the chocolate-dipped side with cocoa powder to serve.

TWICE BAKED JAM AND CUSTARD CROISSANTS WITH MERINGUE

MAKES 6 PASTRIES

6 x 1–2 day old pastries
1 x quantity of Simple Syrup (see page 205)
180g (6¼ oz) jam of your choice
300g (11 oz) Crème Pâtissière (see page 202)

Quick meringue
1 medium egg white
200g (7 oz) icing sugar
a few drops of fresh lemon juice

1. Preheat the oven to 180ºC/350ºF/gas mark 4. Line a baking tray with parchment.

2. Use a small knife to make a hole in the top centre of each croissant. Wiggle a finger inside the hole to make room then dip the croissant in the syrup and place on a lined tray. Pipe 30g (1 oz) of jam and 50g (2 oz) crème pâtissière into each hole.

3. Bake the croissants for 25–30 minutes, turning the tray halfway through. They

should be lightly caramelised underneath and golden on top. Allow to cool a little.

4. Whisk the meringue ingredients together with a handheld electric mixer in a small bowl until the meringue is holding its shape in soft peaks.

5. When the croissants are cool, spread a little meringue along the top and brown with a blow torch or under a preheated hot grill until caramelised, before serving.

TWICE BAKED LEMON CURD AND PISTACHIO CROISSANTS

MAKES 6 PASTRIES

6 x 1–2 day old pastries
1 x quantity of Simple Syrup (see page 205)
180g (6¼ oz) Lemon Curd (see page 205)
1 x quantity of Pistachio Frangipane (see page 203)
30g (1 oz) toasted, chopped pistachios
icing sugar, for dusting

1. Preheat the oven to 180ºC/350ºF/gas mark 4. Line a baking tray with parchment.

2. Slice the croissants through the centre, horizontally, so the pastry opens up like a sandwich. Dip the cut-side of both halves in the syrup and place cut-side up on the lined tray. Pipe or spoon 30g (1 oz) lemon curd and 30g (1 oz) pistachio frangipane

inside each croissant. Place 20g (oz) frangipane and some of the pistachios on top before baking.

3. Bake the croissants for 25–30 minutes, turning the tray halfway through until they are lightly caramelised underneath and golden on top. Allow to cool a little and dust with icing sugar before serving.

TWICE BAKED TAHINI AND CARAMEL CROISSANTS

MAKES 6 PASTRIES

6 x 1–2 day old pastries
1 x quantity of Simple Syrup (see page 205)
1 x quantity of Tahini Frangipane (see page 203)
1kg (2¼ lb) granulated sugar
100g (3½ oz) water
30g (1 oz) toasted sesame seeds

1. Heat the oven to 180ºC/350ºF/gas mark 4. Line a baking tray with parchment.

2. Make a hole in the centre of the top of each croissant with a small knife. Wiggle a clean finger around in the hole to make room then dip the whole croissant briefly in the syrup and place on the tray. Pipe 50g (2 oz) of frangipane into each hole.

3. Bake the croissants for 25–30 minutes, turning halfway through. They should be lightly caramelised underneath and golden on top. Allow to cool.

4. Prepare a bowl of iced water. Bring the sugar and water to the boil rapidly in a small saucepan without stirring until it turns a deep golden brown (don't let it turn too dark or it will taste bitter). Plunge the base of the saucepan into the iced water, then, using tongs, dip each croissant into the caramel and sprinkle with sesame seeds. Alternatively, place the croissants on a wire rack, placed on a sheet of baking parchment, pour the caramel over the top and sprinkle with the sesame seeds.

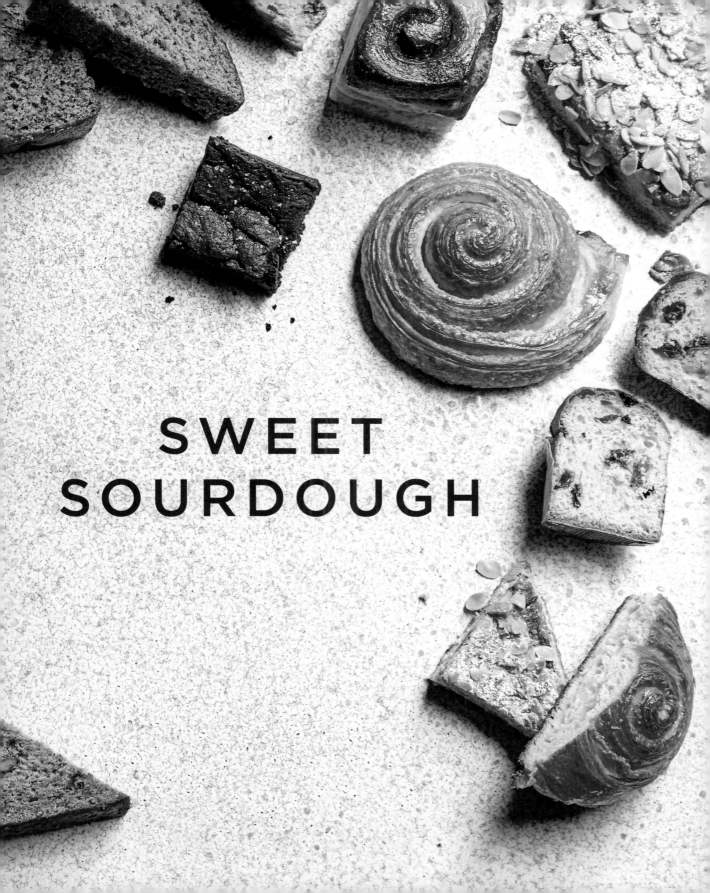

SWEET
SOURDOUGH

SOURDOUGH PANCAKES

My boys ask me for pancakes as often as I am at home at breakfast time, which is relatively infrequently given early starts at the bakery. If the preparation stage is completed the day before they are quick to get on the table in the morning, and the flour is fully hydrated so even with whole wheat these are incredibly light and soft. Sourdough pancakes are the best way to use your starter if the optimum moment for making bread has passed, or for using your brand new starter when you want some instant (in sourdough terms!) gratification, before it is at full strength for making bread.

The timings for this recipe are flexible and can be adjusted by a couple of hours, so take them as a guide. This is designed as an all-in-one jug mix – all the ingredients get added to the same jug through the stages of the recipe, which helps keeps it simple.

MAKES 10–12 PANCAKES

Stage 1: Refreshment
50g (2 oz) whole milk
50g (2 oz) whole wheat flour
5g (⅛ oz) starter (12–24 hours after last refreshment)
1 tsp caster sugar

Stage 2: Refreshment
200g (7 oz) whole milk
10g (¼ oz) caster sugar
100g (3½ oz) plain white flour

Stage 3 Batter mix
60g (2½ oz) unsalted butter
100g (3½ oz)/2 whole eggs, beaten
10g (¼ oz) caster sugar
5g (⅛ oz) bicarbonate of soda
large pinch of sea salt
fresh fruit and maple syrup, to serve

1. Place all the stage 1 ingredients in a 1 litre (1¾ pint) jug large enough to take all the ingredients for the full recipe. Mix, cover and leave in a warm place for 6–10 hours.

2. Add all the stage 2 ingredients to the jug containing the stage 1 starter, mix well to combine. Cover, place in the fridge and allow to ferment for 10–16 hours.

3. Melt 10g (¼ oz) of the butter for stage 3 in a large non-stick frying pan. Add the melted butter to the batter with the remaining stage 3 ingredients, mix until fully combined. The batter should be bubbling as the bicarbonate of soda reacts with the natural acids in the sourdough mixture.

4. Melt the remaining butter in the frying pan and pour into a small jug (this is for frying the pancakes). Heat the frying pan over a high heat until quite hot and then reduce the heat to low. Pour a few drops of the reserved, melted butter into the frying pan, and then pour in enough batter to make a pancake around 12cm (4¾ in) diameter. Cook for around 1½ minutes until the underside is golden brown and the top is starting to look dry and set. Flip the pancake and cook the second side for another minute or so. Transfer to a plate. Continue until all the batter is used up.

5. Serve with fresh fruit and maple syrup.

CRUMPETS

This is essentially a delicious way to eat fermented sourdough starter. I don't think I had eaten a crumpet for twenty years before making my own and don't think I would ever eat another again unless they were home made. There are many good recipes around and sourdough makes them especially delicious.

Eat the crumpets fresh from the pan or allow to cool and toast them. They might not be quite so spongy as the supermarket version but the flavour is much better and they soak up butter just as well. Patience is the key when frying them; don't turn up the heat too high or flip them too soon. I find the bubbles forming and popping mesmerising; crumpets have an excellent effort-to-satisfaction ratio and are a good use for excess starter.

MAKES 10 CRUMPETS

Stage 1: Refreshment
191g (6¾ oz) strong white
bread flour
325g (11½ oz) whole milk
96g (3½ oz) wheat starter at
60% hydration (12–24 hours
after last refreshment)
38g (1½ oz) caster sugar

Stage 2: Batter mix
5g (⅛ oz) caster sugar
2g (⅛ oz) sea salt
3g (⅛ oz) bicarbonate of soda
50g (2 oz) unsalted butter,
for frying

1. Place all the stage 1 ingredients in a 1.5 litre (2¾ pint) jar or jug, mix and cover and leave in the fridge for 10–14 hours. Remove the batter from the fridge and leave at room temperature for 3–4 hours. Alternatively, don't chill the batter but just leave it at room temperature for 4–6 hours.

2. Half an hour before you want to fry the crumpets add the sugar, salt and bicarbonate of soda for stage 2 to the jug and stir well. The acid in the starter will react with the bicarbonate of soda and produce lovely bubbles.

3. Lightly grease the inside of 10cm (4 in) crumpet rings with butter. Heat a large, flat, non-stick frying pan that will fit at least 2 rings inside, over a low to medium heat. When the pan is hot, put the rings in the pan and place a small piece of butter in each ring. Pour approximately 60g (2½ oz) of batter into each ring. Push the batter to the edges of the ring with a spoon if needed they should be about half full. If you have tall rings you could make bigger crumpets – use approximately 100g (3½ oz) batter per ring.

4. During frying, the batter should start to rise in the rings and bubbles will form and pop. When the tops no longer look wet and the crumpets are fully cooked through, remove the rings and flip the crumpets to briefly fry the tops or remove from pan and cool on a wire cooling rack to toast later (this should take 6–7 minutes). They should be golden brown on the bottom – keep peeking at the bottom as they fry and adjust the temperature up or down as needed. I often do a test version on its own first to get a feel for the correct heat of the pan. Fry all the crumpets once you begin so the batter doesn't lose its vigour and liquifies.

5. These are best eaten straight from the pan with butter and jam or honey. Alternatively, they can be frozen on the day that they are cooked.

PLUM AND FENNEL BOSTOCK

Bostock came about as a way to use up the trimmings created during the process of laminating the sourdough pastry dough. We gather them together and bake loaves which are then sliced the following day and turned into bostock. The croissant dough with just some of the butter in it makes a relatively light dough with a closed crumb so it is a good base for topping with fruit and frangipane.

Bostock is also known as brioche aux amandes and the classic version is made with a simple orange infused syrup brushed over slices of day old brioche, topped with almond cream and baked. At Margot we like to be generous with the fruit and to change the flavour with the seasons. There are endless combinations. This recipe uses frangipane and our Plum and fennel jam, but you could use your favourite jam instead.

MAKES 5 PASTRIES

1 x 500–600g Brioche loaf (see page 32 for dough recipe)
300g (11 oz) Almond Frangipane (see page 203)
150g (5 oz) Plum and Fennel Oven Jam (see page 211)
50g (2 oz) flaked almonds

For the syrup
140g (4½ oz) granulated sugar
70g (2¾ oz) water
1 vanilla pod, split and scraped, or a few drops of vanilla extract (optional)

1. For the syrup, place the sugar, water and vanilla pod and seeds (if using) in a small saucepan over a low heat, stirring occasionally. When the liquid is clear and the sugar has dissolved, bring to the boil and then remove from the heat. Set aside to cool and store in the fridge until needed.

2. Preheat the oven to 180ºC/350ºF/gas mark 4. Line a baking tray with baking parchment.

3. Trim the crusts from all sides of the brioche loaf and cut the loaf into 5 slices. Place the brioche slices on the lined tray.

4. Add the extract to the syrup, if using and dip each slice in syrup, making sure the edges of the slices get extra syrup as they are most exposed in the oven. If the brioche is more than one day old or quite dry, then be more generous with the syrup.

5. Spread one fifth of the jam onto each slice of brioche, using the back of a spoon, to spread it almost to the edges.

6. Top each brioche slice with one fifth of the frangipane and use a palette knife to spread the frangipane right to the edges of the slice of brioche.

7. Sprinkle with the flaked almonds and bake for 25–30 minutes. The top should be lightly golden brown and the underside of the brioche should be caramelised lightly on the tray. If they are pale on the bottom and look too wet then bake for a little longer. A contrast of crunchy top and bottom and squidgy centre is what you are aiming for here. Allow to cool for 15–20 minutes before serving or serve at room temperature.

BABKA

The first time I made babka it was for a Rosh Hashanah dinner with friends. Never being one to allow an opportunity to try multiple new recipes to pass I had made four desserts, but it was the babka that everyone loved and this is true at the bakery too. It is our most photographed, ordered and talked about product. Our Jewish customers may recognize it from their family recipes or the versions tasted in New York bakeries, and our Eastern European customers know it by other names but associate it with family celebrations and home. Others have never heard of it and it's a pleasure to bring it to a wider audience.

The flavour of a sourdough babka is complex; balancing sweetness with sour, the soft interior with generous swirls of filling contrasts with the caramelised and sticky outer crust. Make it as a birthday cake, make it for breakfast, tea or as a spectacular – though not light – pudding; but do make it. Your guests will love you for it.

MAKES 1 BABKA
1.35kg (3 lb)

1 x quantity of Brioche dough
(complete the recipe on page
32 up until the dough goes
into the fridge)
flour, for dusting
filling of your choice
1 x quantity of Simple Syrup
(see page 205)

1. Line a 10 x 30cm (4x11¾ in) loaf tin or a 25cm (10 in) round cake tin with baking parchment.

2. Remove the brioche dough from the fridge and lay on a lightly floured surface. Push the dough into a rough rectangle shape and roll until approximately 20 x 40cm (8 x 16 in) and 3–5mm (⅛–¼ in) thick. The bigger the rectangle, the more swirls of filling will be in your dough.

3. Spread the filling over the dough, right to the edges on three sides but leaving a 1cm (½ in) border with no filling on one short end of the rectangle.

4. From the short side covered to the edge, roll up the dough in a tight roll, finishing where the border is. Seal the seam by pinching the dough together and place on the work surface with the seam side down, and a short side facing you.

5. Cut the roll through the middle lengthways with a dough cutter or sharp knife. You will have two long halves with the lines of filling exposed in the middle.

6. Cross the pieces over each other in an X shape – the cut side with the lines should be facing upwards. Twist the two bottom halves of the X around each other from the middle to the end and do the same on the other side. Try to keep the cut side with the lines facing upwards as you shape. Re-shape with your hands into a fat, even loaf. If you're using a round tin, roll a larger rectangle and roll up from the long side, then coil the braided babka into a circle.

7. Place the babka into the lined tin and allow it to proof for 16–24 hours in a warm place at around 24ºC (75ºF).

8. Twenty minutes before baking, preheat the oven to 200ºC/400ºF/gas mark 6. Place a metal roasting tin in the oven to preheat.

9. Place the babka in the oven and pour 150–200ml (5–7 fl oz) water into the roasting tin. Reduce the heat to 180ºC/350ºF/gas mark 4 and then bake for 30 minutes. Remove the roasting tin from the oven and bake the babka for a further 15–25 minutes or until the internal temperature is 98ºC (208ºF) and a skewer inserted into the centre comes out clean (it may be sticky with the filling however). Soak with the syrup.

FILLINGS

CHOCOLATE

In a medium heatproof bowl place 30g
(1 oz) cocoa powder, 160g (5½ oz)
chopped dark chocolate and 40g (1½ oz)
date syrup. Heat 140g (4½ oz) unsalted
butter until melted and bubbling and pour
over the chocolate mixture. Stand for
5 minutes and then stir. Some lumps may
remain but it doesn't matter. Cool for
30–60 minutes before spreading over the
dough. It should be spreadable but not
runny. If it sets before you use it, place
the bowl over a pan of gently simmering
water and stir.

CHOCOLATE AND RASPBERRY

Make the chocolate filling, as above,
and after you have spread it over the
dough top with 150g (5 oz) fresh or
frozen raspberries.

CINNAMON BABKA

Chop 185g (6½ oz) unsalted butter
into small cubes and set aside at room
temperature, for 10–20 minutes, to
soften. Place 45g (1½ oz) dark brown
sugar and 45g (1½ oz) caster sugar in a
bowl with 15g (½ oz) ground cinnamon,
stir to combine. Stir the butter into the
sugar and cinnamon. Spread evenly
over the dough.

POPPY SEED BABKA

Place 100g (3½ oz) poppy seeds in a
medium pan of water, bring to the boil
and simmer for 1 hour. Drain the poppy
seeds and set aside to cool in a medium
mixing bowl. Stir 200g (7 oz) crème
pâtissière (see page 202) into the poppy
seeds with the finely grated zest of 1 small
orange and ½ tsp vanilla extract. Spread
evenly over the dough.

CINNAMON BUNS

We bake cinnamon buns every day and always make slightly more than we think we will sell because they double up as the base for the Apple and Cinnamon Bread and Butter Pudding the next day. We have a wonderful frame for baking our buns in the shop made by Campbell who is a metal fabricator and talented amateur baker. He dreams up designs that solve problems bakers all over the world didn't know they had and finds ways to make large-scale baking easier. The buns can also be batch baked where they touch each other in the tin to be torn apart while still warm. The filling is not overly sweet because too much sugar slows down the fermentation of the dough. They are soaked in syrup after baking so don't need too much sugar in the filling anyway.

While we use the same dough and filling for babka and cinnamon buns, the end result and the crust to crumb ratio is quite different, so customers still prefer one or the other.

MAKES 9 BUNS

1 x quantity of Brioche dough (complete the recipe on page 32 up until the dough goes into the fridge)
flour, for dusting

For the cinnamon filling
185g (6½ oz) unsalted butter at room temperature, finely cubed
45g (1½ oz) dark brown sugar
45g (1½ oz) caster sugar
15g (½ oz) ground cinnamon

1 x quantity of Simple Syrup (see page 205)

1. Line a 23cm (9 in) square tin with baking parchment.

2. Remove the brioche dough from the fridge and lay on a lightly floured surface. Push the dough into a rough rectangle shape and roll into a 20 x 27cm (8 x 10¾ in) rectangle. The longer edges of the rectangle should be at the top and bottom on the work surface.

3. Combine the butter, sugars and cinnamon in a bowl. Spread the filling over the dough leaving a 1cm border with no filling at the top long edge, of the rectangle.

4. Mark 3cm (1¼ in) increments along the bottom long edge of the rectangle and cut the dough vertically into 9 strips, each 3 x 20cm (1¼ x 8 in) long. Don't separate them.

5. Roll 3 strips at a time; rolling from the bottom of the strips to the top and then separate them. Lay them, swirl side down, in the tin in 3 rows of 3.

6. Cover the tin with clingfilm and allow it to rest for 16–24 hours in a warm place at around 24ºC (75ºF).

7. Twenty minutes before baking, preheat the oven to 200ºC/400ºF/gas mark 6. Place a metal roasting tin in the oven to preheat.

8. Place the cinnamon buns in the oven and pour 150–200ml (5–7 fl oz) water into the roasting tin. Reduce the heat to 180ºC/350ºF/gas mark 4 and bake for 15 minutes. Remove the roasting tin from the oven. Bake the rolls for a further 15–20 minutes or until the internal temperature is 98ºC (208ºF) and a skewer inserted into the centre comes out clean .

9. When the rolls come out of the oven, soak with the syrup. Cool in the tin.

SWEET SOURDOUGH

APPLE AND CINNAMON BREAD AND BUTTER PUDDING

Marta worked at Margot from the first day we opened on 14 February 2016; I interviewed her amongst the piles of boxes while the builders finished the last of the works. The plan was that she would work part time as a barista and possibly make some pastry, in the future, as she had experience in both. But even before we opened it was clear that the bakery needed her pastry skills most of all and she became the full time pastry chef within three weeks. Marta baked the first cake to sit on the Margot counter and met every challenge that came our way in those first two years with loyalty, hard work and resilience. She has since left to continue her training back home in Italy but many recipes make me think of her and this is one that she developed. I thought customers would not want to eat bread and butter pudding at the height of summer but apparently they do and we bake it every day, year round; it's a light and not too sweet custard over leftover cinnamon buns with apple. So simple and so good.

MAKES 1 PUDDING
20cm (8in)

750g (1 lb 11 oz) cinnamon buns or alternative (see box)
380–400g (13¼–14 oz) apples (we like Cox's, Discovery or Bramley)
285g (10 oz)/6 whole eggs, beaten
125ml (4 fl oz) double cream
75g (3 oz) caster or vanilla sugar
1 tsp vanilla extract (optional)
375g (13 oz) whole milk
50g (2 oz) Demerara sugar

1. Line a 20cm (8 in) square tin with baking parchment. Preheat the oven to 180ºC/350ºF/gas mark 4.

2. Slice the cinnamon buns into 3–4cm (1¼–1½ in) thick slices. Core and roughly slice the apples.

3. Place a layer of cinnamon buns in the lined tin (around half the slices), making sure they reach the corners of the tin fully. Scatter with half the apple slices.

4. Place the eggs, cream, caster or vanilla sugar and vanilla, if using, in a medium heatproof bowl and whisk until well combined.

5. Heat the milk in a small pan and bring to the boil. Pour the hot milk immediately over the egg mixture, whisking constantly as you pour.

6. Pour half the custard mix over the buns and apple in the tin. Arrange the remaining buns in the tin, top with the remaining apple and pour over the remaining custard. Use the back of a spoon to firmly push down on the ingredients – the apple should be submerged in custard and the buns fully soaked.

7. Sprinkle with the Demerara sugar and bake in the oven for 50–70 minutes – the longer you bake it for the firmer set your custard will be. The apples and Demerara should be caramelised and crispy in places.

8. Allow to cool and stand for at least 30 minutes before serving warm. It can be stored in the fridge for up to one day.

ALTERNATIVES TO CINNAMON BUNS

Instead of cinnamon buns, use any leftover sweet pastries or sliced panettone. For a traditional bread and butter pudding, you can, of course, use bread – slice it thinly, remove the crusts and spread with butter and to add extra sweetness double the quantity of sugar in the custard.

BRIOCHE FEUILLETÉE

My French should be better than it is but with a French-speaking husband this just made me lazy as on our trips to Paris to visit his grandmother, he could ask for anything I needed and I could only offer a badly accented 'Hello' and 'Thank you'. So I cannot pronounce or spell this pastry without some effort; I'm tempted to go with the more prosaic Australian 'snails' at times. It is flaky brioche; as if brioche did not already have enough butter, one laminates it again and the pastries come out ethereally light. They are beautiful in their simplicity; crispy, squidgy swirls of plain but rich pastry. If you wanted to make them more elaborate, spreading the dough with Sicilian pistachio crème or a sprinkle of pearl sugar before rolling them up would be a suitable embellishment.

MAKES 12 FEUILLETÉE

1 x quantity of Brioche dough (complete the recipe on page 32 up until the dough goes into the fridge and chill for 4–5 hours or overnight) 300g (11 oz) unsalted butter 200g (7 oz) simple syrup (see page 205)

1. Prepare the butter block following the steps outlined on page 82.

2. Following the instructions on page 205, prepare the syrup. You will need a little of it at the shaping stage and the remainder after baking. Store in the fridge in the meantime.

3. Follow lamination instructions as for the Croissants on page 80–81 with a rest in between.

4. Chill the dough after the final lamination and rest for a further 2 hours in the fridge or overnight to shape the following day.

5. Remove the dough from the fridge. Roll the dough into a 30cm (12 in) square on a lightly floured surface. Trim the edges of the dough to expose the lamination.

6. Mark the bottom of the square, to divide it vertically into 10 equal pieces, 3cm (1¼ in) wide. Brush the top of the strips with a little syrup; this helps hold the pastries together without unravelling. Cut the strips and roll up together 3 or 4 at a time. Lay, swirl-side down, on a lined baking tray with 7.5–10cm (3–4 in) between each one. Use two trays if needed.

7. Allow the shaped dough to rest for 16–24 hours in a warm place, at around 24ºC (75ºF).

8. Preheat the oven to 220ºC/425ºF/gas mark 7. Place a metal roasting tin in the oven to preheat.

9. Place the swirls in the oven, add steam (see Baking Instructions on page 23) and immediately reduce the oven temperature to 200ºC/400ºF/gas mark 6. Bake for 15 minutes and reduce the temperature to 180ºC/350ºF/gas mark 4. Remove the steam tin and turn the baking tray(s) in the oven. Bake for another 10–15 minutes until the pastries have a deep golden colour, tinged brown at the edges. They shouldn't look burnt but you want some colour so the pastry still has substance after it has been soaked with syrup.

10. Brush generously with syrup, it isn't a glaze here – it should soak into the pastries until they are as sweet as they are buttery. Store in an airtight container for up to 3 days.

HOT CROSS BUNS

I confess a fondness for hot cross buns undimmed by conversion to Judaism. We make them as we have customers of many faiths and backgrounds and because I believe that it is best to focus on sharing food and celebrations whenever we may have the chance in a shared community space. As I don't bake them at home, the bakery gives me the chance to savour the process and the flavour and to bring the beauty of the sourdough version to an appreciative audience when demand is highest. I can't bring myself to cross them in the traditional way however – it seems one step too far – so I cross them but in the manner of a game of naughts and crosses, with an X, corner to corner. A nod to the tradition and a little personal distance from it.

MAKES 12 BUNS

Stage 1: Refreshment
20g (¾ oz) strong white
bread flour
20g (¾ oz) water
10g (¼ oz) whole wheat
starter (8–12 hours after last
refreshment)

Stage 2: Refreshment
90g (3¼ oz) bread flour
53g (2 oz) water
20g (¾ oz) caster sugar

For the fruit mix
184g (6½ oz) raisins
103g (3½ oz) cranberries
34g (1¼ oz) mincemeat or
17g (½ oz) brandy mixed
with 17g (½ oz) plum jam
½ tsp ground cinnamon
½ tsp caraway seeds
zest of half an orange

Stage 3: Dough mix
207g (7¼ oz) whole milk
459g (1lb ¼ oz) strong
white bread flour, plus extra
for dusting
98g (3½ oz)/2 whole eggs,
beaten
96g (3½ oz) caster sugar
10g (¼ oz) sea salt

continued overleaf

1. Place all the stage 1 ingredients in a 1 litre (1¾ pint) Kilner jar or container with a lid, mix, cover and leave at warm room temperature for 8–12 hours.

2. Combine the stage 2 ingredients with 45g (1½ oz) of the stage 1 mix in a Kilner jar. Stir together and then cover and leave at warm room temperature for 10–14 hours.

3. Combine all the fruit mix ingredients in a bowl, stir well and leave, covered at room temperature until you are ready to add to the dough.

4. Place the flour, eggs, very slightly warmed milk, sugar and salt with 207g (7¼ oz) of starter in the bowl of a free standing mixer fitted with a dough hook; mix for 5 minutes on a low speed. Scrape down the sides, mix on a medium speed for 5 minutes. Cover and leave for 30 minutes.

5. Add the butter, a cube at a time, to the dough mix and mix for 5 minutes on a low speed and another 5 minutes on a medium speed. Add the fruit mix and mix on the lowest speed for 1–2 minutes until just incorporated into the dough.

6. Use the sunflower oil to grease a large bowl or a rectangular flat bottomed glass or plastic container with a capacity of at least 3 litres (5¼ pints). Transfer the dough to the bowl or container, cover and rest in a warm place for 2–3 hours. Then transfer to the fridge and chill the dough for 1–2 hours before shaping, to make the dough easier to handle.

7. Line a 25 x 30cm (10 x 12 in) baking tray with baking parchment. Divide your dough into 12 x 120g (3¾ oz) pieces. Dust your hand and the top of one piece of dough with flour. Place on the work surface. Using small circular motions allow it to come into a tight round in the palm of your hand.

8. Place the buns in the lined tin in 3 rows of 4. They should have some space between them but should touch once they begin to proof. Place in the fridge for 8 to 24 hours.

9. Remove the buns from the fridge and proof for 8–12 hours in a warm place, around 24ºC (75ºF), until they are puffy and touching each other in the tin.

continued overleaf

96g (3½ oz) unsalted butter, chilled and cut into 2.5cm (1 in) pieces

sunflower oil, for greasing

For the syrup

100g (3½ oz) granulated sugar

50g (2 oz) water

1 vanilla pod, split and scraped

For the crossing paste

40g (1½ oz) white bread flour

15g (½ oz) whole milk

20g (¾ oz) caster sugar

20g (¾ oz) unsalted butter, melted

10g (¼ oz) whole egg

10. For the syrup, place the sugar, water and vanilla pod and seeds in a small saucepan over a low heat, stir occasionally. When the liquid is clear and the sugar has dissolved, bring to the boil and then remove from the heat. Set aside to cool and store in the fridge until needed.

11. For the crossing paste, mix all the ingredients together in a small bowl until well combined. The mix should be thick enough to hold a line when piped on the buns but not too stiff. Add a few more drops of milk if needed.

12. Twenty minutes before baking, preheat the oven to 180°C/350°F/gas mark 4 and place a metal roasting tin in the oven to preheat.

13. Pipe the crossing paste in lines across the buns; a single line of paste should go from one end of the tin to the other over the centre of the buns. They don't need to be individually crossed.

14. Place the buns in the oven and pour 150–200ml (5–7 fl oz) water into the roasting tin. Bake for 20 minutes, turn the tray and remove the roasting tin from the oven. Bake for another 15 minutes, until the internal temperature is 98°C (208°F) and a skewer inserted into the centre comes out clean. The buns should be golden on top.

15. Brush the hot buns, in the tin, with a generous amount of syrup. Eat warm or transfer to a wire rack to cool and store in an airtight container for up to 3 days. They are also excellent toasted, when a day or two old.

DOUGHNUTS

My parents are from Manchester and I grew up in Australia eating potatoes with most meals and homemade chips fried in a chip pan, to the bemusement of my Australian friends. The only person I know who still fries chips in a chip pan is my Nana. I never much embraced frying once I lived alone. I'm not sure it would be good for me to have unlimited access to homemade chips, not being much for self deprivation, so I fry food once a year during Chanukah but do so in spectacular style with homemade latkes and doughnuts; it's the point at which the two parts of my life collide in a fug of hot oil.

At the bakery we only make sourdough doughnuts for the 8 days of Chanukah, lacking sufficient extraction, space or time to do them year round. Rolling, proofing, frying and filling hundreds of these lovely sweets is hard on all the bakers already overloaded with numerous pre-Christmas tasks and orders but we make and fry them, because what's a Jewish bakery without doughnuts at Chanukah?

This dough would require a lot of effort to develop by hand though it could be done with time and patience. I recommend using a free standing mixer.

MAKES 15 DOUGHNUTS

Stage 1: Refreshment
17g (½ oz) strong white bread flour
17g (½ oz) water
8g (¼ oz) whole wheat starter (8–12 hours after last refreshment

Stage 2: Refreshment
84g (3¼ oz) strong white bread flour
51g (2 oz) water
21g (¾ oz) caster sugar

Stage 3: Dough mix
421g (15 oz) strong white bread flour plus extra for dusting
174g (6 oz)/3½ whole eggs, beaten
112g (4 oz) water
124g (4 oz) sugar
9g (¼ oz) sea salt
75g (3 oz) unsalted butter, chilled and cut into 2.5cm (1 in) cubes
rice flour, for dusting
500g (1 lb 2 oz) caster sugar, for coating
4 litres (7 pints) sunflower oil

1. Place all the stage 1 ingredients in a 1 litre (1¾ pint) jar or container with a lid, cover, mix and leave at warm room temperature for 8–12 hours.

2. Place the flour, water and sugar for stage 2 starter in the jar containing the stage 1 starter, mix, cover and leave at warm room temperature for 10–14 hours.

3. Combine the flour, eggs and 90g (3¼ oz) of the water for stage 3 and 177g (6 oz) of the starter in the bowl of a free standing mixer fitted with a dough hook; mix for 5 minutes on a low speed. Scrape down the sides, mix on a medium speed for 5 minutes. Cover and leave for 30 minutes.

4. Add the sugar and salt to the mixer bowl and mix for 5 minutes on a low speed and another 5 minutes on a medium speed. Begin to add the butter, one piece at a time, over the next 5 minutes with the mixer running on a low speed, allow each piece to be absorbed into the dough before adding the next piece. Add the remaining 22g (¾ oz) of water to the dough.

5. Scrape down the sides regularly and mix for another 10 minutes after the butter has been incorporated. The exact length of time will depend on the power of your mixer. The dough is ready when you can stretch it with your fingers into a thin, transparent window and a hole poked in the window has clean, rather than jagged edges.

6. Use the sunflower oil to grease a large mixing bowl or rectangular flat bottomed glass or plastic container with a capacity of at least 2 litres (3½ pints). Transfer the dough to the bowl or container, cover and rest for 2 hours at room temperature.

7. Fold the dough four times, leaving 30 minutes between each fold. Leave the dough in a warm place, around 24ºC (75ºF), for 7–10 hours. Transfer the dough to the fridge for 12–18 hours.

continued overleaf

8. When you are ready to fry the doughnuts, remove the dough from the fridge. Dust a tray with rice flour. Divide the dough into 15 x 65g (2½ oz) pieces and shape them into rounds on the work surface, with a lightly floured hand. Place on the dusted tray to rest for 30–60 minutes.

9. Place the caster sugar in a bowl. Line a tray with kitchen paper. Add the oil to a large, heavy-based saucepan or deep fat fryer so that it is two thirds full. Heat the oil to 170°C (338°F).

10. When the oil is ready, remove the doughnuts from the tray using a dough scraper and carefully lower into the oil, using a slotted spoon. Fry in batches of 4–6, depending on the size of your pan. Cook for 2–3 minutes on one side, turn in the oil and give them another 1–2 minutes until golden and cooked through – they are ready when until the internal temperature is 98°C (208°F) and a skewer inserted into the centre comes out clean.

11. Remove from the pan using a slotted spoon and place on sheets of kitchen paper, to drain and cool for 1 minute. Toss the doughnuts in the caster sugar. Best eaten immediately, or allow to cool before filling.

TO FILL DOUGHNUTS

Jam, lemon curd (see page 205), plain or chocolate crème pâtissière (see page 202) all work well as fillings for the doughnuts. To make chocolate crème pâtissière, fold 20g (¾ oz) melted, cooled chocolate into 100g (3½ oz) crème pâtissière along with 50g (2 oz) lightly whipped cream.
Put your choice of filling into a large piping bag fitted with nozzle. Cut a hole in the side of the doughnut with a small sharp knife and squeeze as much filling as possible into the centre.

PANETTONE

Panettone is one of the few breads still naturally leavened in its modern form; there are yeast versions to make and buy but the process of making panettone has not been lost to time. This is not to say that it is easy. On the contrary, I can hardly think of a more challenging process more likely to go wrong in a myriad of ways. Bakers like a challenge though and I have seen renewed enthusiasm for panettone online in the three years since we started making it at Margot. When it works it is incredibly satisfying; the primary goals are to achieve a sweet flavour and an open, light crumb, distinct from cake or a bread, with fruit. It should hold its shape after baking and last for a long time. It's also a fantastic base for Apple Bread and Butter Pudding (see page 119) should you have any left over. Focus on the strength of your starter; success flows from there. This recipe takes 8 days to make.

MAKES 1 LOAF
800g (1¾ lb)

Stage 1: Refreshment
50g (2 oz) strong white
bread flour
20g (¾ oz) water
10g (¼ oz) wheat starter
(12 hours after last refreshment)

Stage 2: Refreshment
50g (2 oz) strong white
bread flour
20g (¾ oz) water
10g (¼ oz) stage 1 starter 4
hours after final refreshment

Stage 3: First dough mix
69g (2½)/5 egg yolks
68g (2½ oz) caster sugar
213g (7½ oz) strong white
bread flour
80g (3 oz) water
76g (3 oz) unsalted butter, at
room temperature and cut into
2.5cm (1 in) cubes
sunflower oil, for greasing

Stage 4: Second dough mix
69g (2½)/5 egg yolks
13g (½ oz) sugar
53g (2 oz) strong white bread
flour plus extra for dusting
5g (⅛ oz) sea salt
82g (3 oz) unsalted butter, at
room temperature, cut into
2.5cm (1 in) cubes

continued overleaf

1. Mix all the stage 1 ingredients in a 200ml (7 fl oz) jar or container with a lid, cover and leave at warm room temperature for 12 hours. Repeat this refreshment schedule twice a day, every 12 hours, for 3 or 4 days in the days before you start the more concentrated refreshments ready for mixing.

2. The day before you mix the first dough, refresh your starter 5 times, every 4 hours with the stage 2 refreshment just before you go to bed.

3. The morning of the day you will mix the first dough, refresh the starter twice; once as soon as you wake up and again 4 hours later – this will be the levain that goes into your first dough. Wait four more hours and then mix into your first dough.

4. To make the first dough: mix together the egg yolk and sugar for the stage 3 dough mix in a small bowl. Have all the other ingredients for the stage 3 dough weighed out and ready in separate bowls. Combine one third of the egg and sugar mix and one third of the water for the stage 3 dough with the flour and all the starter in the bowl of a free standing mixer fitted with a dough hook; mix for 5 minutes on a low speed. Scrape down the sides, add another third of the water and the egg and sugar mix and mix again for 5 minutes.

5. Add the remaining egg, sugar and water and mix for 10 minutes on a medium speed. Add the butter, a cube at a time, over the final 5–10 minutes of the mix. The dough should be smooth and strong at the end of the mix.

6. Use the sunflower oil to grease a rectangular flat bottomed glass or plastic container with a capacity of at least 1 litre (1¾ pints). Transfer the dough to the container, cover and mark the level of the dough on the side so you can check when the dough has tripled in volume. Place the dough in a warm place, around 24–28°C (75–82°F), for 12–24 hours.

7. When the dough has tripled in volume you can mix the stage 4 dough. Place the stage 3 dough in the bowl of a free standing mixer fitted with the dough hook. Mix the egg yolks and sugar for the stage 4 dough in a small bowl and add half to the bowl with half the water and all the flour for the second dough. Mix for 5 minutes on a medium speed.

8. Add the remaining egg and sugar and mix for 5 minutes. Add the salt to the dough and then the butter, a cube at a time, while you mix for 5–10 minutes on a medium speed. Add the remaining water and mix until incorporated into the

continued overleaf

For the fruit and flavourings
117g (4 oz) raisins
117g (4 oz) candied peel
finely grated zest of ½ orange
seeds from ½ vanilla pod

dough. The dough should be strong and smooth; stretch a small amount between your fingers and if you can form a thin 'window' that breaks with clean lines to the edge when you poke a hole in it then it is ready. Add the fruit and flavourings to the dough and mix for 3–5 minutes on a low speed until well mixed.

9. Remove the dough from the mixer bowl and pre-shape into a round (see page 21–22). Lightly dust the top of your dough with flour and leave to rest for 30 minutes.

10. Follow the instructions on pages 21–22 shape the dough as for a round loaf of bread and place seam-side down in the paper case.

11. Place the dough in a warm place, around 24–28ºC (75–82ºF), for 8–20 hours. When it has risen almost to the top or is just poking out of the top edge of the paper it is ready to bake.

12. Preheat the oven to 180ºC/350ºF/gas mark 4.

13. Bake the panettone for 45–55 minutes or until the internal temperature is 93–98ºC (199–208ºF) and a skewer inserted into the centre comes out clean. As soon as it comes out of the oven stick 2 skewers through the base of the paper case – through the panettone and the paper and flip it upside down. This will prevent it from collapsing. Rest in a deep container until cool.

14. Serve fresh or wrap well and keep for up to 3 months.

STOLLEN

This past Christmas one of my customers, Arthur Fleiss, ordered several stollen and sent me a story about his connection with this festive bread. His mother was from Chemnitz, Saxony, where stollen originates and she recalled the preparation of stollen by the family cook in the lead up to Christmas and Chanukah during her childhood in the 1920s. A dozen stollen were walked down to the local bakery on a little wooden handcart to be baked and the loaves were then given as Christmas presents.

It's a story that speaks of connections between people during the festive season and the power of food to imbue memories and endure in the retelling for a hundred years. Arthur's parents became refugees and the community in Chemnitz did not fare well in the years that followed, and so the story is tinged with sadness, too. I shall think of Arthur and his mother whenever I make stollen from now on. I appreciate the stories people share with me at the bakery; it is one of the greatest pleasures and privileges of the role of a baker.

MAKES 2 LOAVES
700g (1 lb 9 oz)

Stage 1: Refreshment
50g (2 oz) strong white
bread flour
20g (¾ oz) water
10g (¼ oz) wheat starter (12
hours after last refreshment)

Stage 2: Refreshment
100g (3½ oz) strong white
bread flour
40g (1½ oz) water
50g (2 oz) stage 1 starter 4
hours after final refreshment

Stage 3: First dough mix
244g (9 oz) flour plus extra for
dusting
104g (3½ oz) whole milk
18g (½ oz) caster sugar
36g (1½ oz) unsalted butter,
chilled and cut into 2.5cm
(1 in) cubes
sunflower oil, for greasing

continued overleaf

1. Mix all the stage 1 ingredients in a 200ml (7fl oz) jar or container with a lid, cover and leave at warm room temperature for 12 hours. Repeat this refreshment schedule twice a day, every 12 hours, for 3 or 4 days in the days before you start the more concentrated refreshments ready for mixing.

2. The day before you mix the first dough, refresh your starter 5 times, every 4 hours with the stage 2 ingredients just before you go to bed.

3. The day you will mix the first dough, refresh the starter every four hours again; adjust the number of refreshments to suit your schedule but mix the first dough 4 hours after your final refreshment

4. Combine the flour, milk and sugar, for stage 3, with 163g (5½ oz) of stage 2 starter in the bowl of free standing mixer fitted with a dough hook. Mix for 5 minutes on a low speed. Scrape down the sides, add the butter to the dough and mix on a medium speed for 5 minutes. The dough is fairly dry and firm and does not need extensive mixing. It can also be kneaded by hand on an unfloured work surface for 7–8 minutes.

5. Use the sunflower oil to grease a rectangular flat bottomed glass or plastic container with a capacity of at least 3 litres (5¼ pints). Transfer the dough to the container, cover and mark the level of the dough on the side, so you can check when the dough has doubled. Place the dough in a cool place for 8–12 hours.

6. Combine the raisins, candied peel, cranberries, rum or hot water, orange zest, caraway seeds, cinnamon and vanilla in a bowl and leave at room temperature while the first dough ferments.

7. Preheat the oven to 180ºC/350ºF/ gas mark 4. Place the nuts on a non-stick baking tray and roast for 5–10 minutes until golden and fragrant. Turn the oven off.

8. When the dough has doubled in volume you can mix the second dough. Place the first dough in the bowl of a free standing mixer fitted with the dough hook. Add the milk, salt and sugar for the stage 4 and mix for 2–3 minutes on a low speed until fully incorporated. Mix for an additional 3–5 minutes while rapidly adding the butter a cube at a time. When the dough

continued overleaf

Additions
120g (4 oz) raisins
50g (2 oz) candied peel
50g (2 oz) dried cranberries
35g (1¼ oz) rum or hot water
finely grated zest of ½ orange
½ tsp caraway seeds
½ tsp ground cinnamon
½ vanilla pod, seeds scraped or
½ tsp vanilla extract
75g (3 oz) whole almonds,
skin on
150g (5 oz) marzipan

Stage 4: Second dough mix
12g (½ oz) whole milk
1 tsp sea salt
36g (1½ oz) sugar
145g (5 oz) unsalted butter, at
room temperature and cut into
2.5cm (1 in) cubes

For the coating
200g (7 oz) unsalted butter
1kg (2¼ lb) icing sugar

is smooth and the ingredients are fully mixed into the dough, add the fruit mixture and almonds and gently mix for 2–3 minutes until incorporated evenly through the dough.

9. Weigh your dough and divide it in half. Pre-shape into rounds, dust the tops with flour and leave to rest on the work surface for 20–30 minutes.

10. Preheat the oven to 180ºC/350ºF/ gas mark 4. Line a baking tray with baking parchment.

11. To shape your dough, turn it over so the top is now touching the work surface. Shape into a rough oval with your hands but don't handle the dough any more than necessary. Roll the marzipan into 2 x 15cm (6 in) 'sausages'. Flour your rolling pin and make an indent in the centre of the dough; lay your 'sausage' of marzipan in the indent and fold the dough over so you have a half circle with the marzipan inside. Find the point on the opposite side to the fold of the dough where the marzipan stops and make another indent here with your rolling pin, effectively sealing the marzipan into the dough and creating a dip in the dough which gives the traditional shape.

12. Gently shape the ends of your loaf into soft points and lay the loaves on the lined trays.

13. Bake for 35–45 minutes until golden or the internal temperature is 93–98ºC (199–208ºF) and a skewer inserted into the thickest part of the dough comes out clean. Set aside to cool on the tray.

14. When the stollen is cool, melt the butter for the coating in a small pan. Brush the stollen all over with melted butter and then liberally dust the top and bottom of the loaf with icing sugar to create a thick coating. Leave to set on a tray for a few hours and then wrap firmly. You can serve straight away but the flavour is best after about a week. Well wrapped it will keep for a month.

15. Serve thin slices with tea. It is meant to be a little dry, though not overly so but don't think of it as a cake so much as a rich, dense bread.

SOURDOUGH BANANA BREAD

When I came to London at the age of 22 after finishing my degree, I was supposed to stay a couple of years or so, work and travel and then go back to Australia, but I have never been quite finished with this city. I lived with a lovely family for my first year and they enjoyed good food and encouraged me to cook, which was mutually beneficial. *How to be a Domestic Goddess* was a book they owned; newly released at the time and a revelation. I thought it old fashioned to be a baker of cakes; I liked to bake but had never once considered it to be a potential career. Encouraged by the appealing recipes and the enthusiastic response from recipients, I baked my way through much of that book and have never stopped returning to my favourite recipes. It is intimately linked with my memories of the time when I found my place here. Nigella's Banana Bread is perfect in its original form with its walnuts and raisins; so when I came to dabble in sourdough cakes I tried various banana cakes but the one I like best is at the beginning, slightly altered and with added fermentation because I can't resist following an idea.

MAKES 1 LOAF
1kg (2¼ lb)

Stage 1: Refreshment
16g (½ oz) strong whole wheat bread flour
16g (½ oz) water
8g (¼ oz) whole wheat starter (8–12 hours after last refreshment)

Stage 2: Refreshment
80g (3 oz) bread flour
48g (1¾ oz) water
20g (¾ oz) caster sugar

Stage 3: First mix
91g (3¼ oz) plain white flour
100g (3½ oz)/2 whole eggs, beaten
71g (2¾ oz) caster sugar
275g (10 oz) mashed banana (3–4 small to medium bananas)
90g (3¼ oz) raisins
60g (2½ oz) water

Stage 4: Second mix
110g (3¾ oz) unsalted butter
71g (2¾ oz) dark brown sugar
½ tsp sea salt
70g (2¾ oz) walnuts (optional)

1. Place all the stage 1 ingredients in a 500ml (17fl oz) jar or container with a lid, mix, cover and leave at warm room temperature for 8–12 hours.

2. Place all the stage 2 ingredients into the 500ml (17fl oz) jar containing the Stage 1 starter, mix, cover and leave at warm room temperature for 12–16 hours.

3. Place all the stage 3 ingredients plus 167g (5¾ oz) of starter in a medium bowl and mix with a whisk until well combined – don't over mix but do make sure the starter is well distributed in the mix. Leave in a warm place at room temperature for 5–6 hours. It should increase in volume by half.

4. Melt the butter for stage 4 in a small pan and set aside to cool. Line a 800g (1¾ lb) loaf tin with baking parchment.

5. If using the walnuts, spread across a tray and toast for 5–10 minutes in oven at 180°C/350°F/gas mark 4.

6. Add the melted butter and remaining stage 4 ingredients to the bowl containing the batter. Mix until well combined with a spatula or wooden spoon but don't overmix.

7. Pour into the lined loaf tin and leave for 3–4 hours until the batter has risen by 1–2cm (¼– ¾ in).

8. Towards the end of the final proofing time for the batter, preheat the oven to 160°C/325°F/gas mark 3.

9. Bake for 45–55 minutes or until a skewer inserted in the centre comes out clean.

10. Cool in the tin for 30 minutes and then turn out onto a wire rack. Slice once it's completely cool. It will be denser than a normal cake raised with baking powder as the flour will have fermented along with all the other ingredients, but it won't taste sour.

SOURDOUGH RYE BROWNIES

Rye has an affinity with chocolate, evidenced by various bakeries across the world making incredibly delicious brownies and cookies using both these ingredients. The first time I came across the combination was in Claire Ptak's Violet Bakery cookbook some years ago, which is the basis for this recipe and what struck me about using rye flour was the danger of failure was vastly reduced; it was a dislike of dry brownies that had more or less put me off making them at all. Rye is low in gluten so is more forgiving than the more commonly used wheat flour which can make brownies dry and tough especially if overbaked. If you ignore the peculiar colour of egg fermenting with rye flour and proceed to the end you will find these brownies a fudgy, sweet and lightly fermented addition to your brownie repertoire and a good use of any spare rye starter – you could use old starter here too instead of making it according to the refreshment schedule below.

MAKES 12 BROWNIES

Stage 1: Refreshment
72g (2¾ oz) wholegrain rye flour
57g (2¼ oz) water
36g (1½ oz) rye or wheat starter (8–12 hours after last refreshment)

Stage 2: First mix
194g (6¾ oz) wholegrain rye flour
250g (9 oz)/5 whole eggs, beaten
100g (3½ oz) caster sugar

Stage 3: Final mix
195g (6¾ oz) unsalted butter
475g (1lb ½ oz) dark chocolate, at least 66% cocoa solids
77g (3 oz) caster sugar
265g (9¼ oz) dark brown sugar
70g (2¾ oz) good quality cocoa powder
5g (⅛ oz) vanilla extract
3g (⅛ oz) bicarbonate of soda
2g (⅛ oz) sea salt, plus extra for sprinkling (optional)

1. Place all the stage 1 ingredients in a 300ml (½ pint) jar or container with a lid, mix, cover and leave at warm room temperature for 4–6 hours

2. Place the stage 2 ingredients plus 125g (4 oz) of the starter in a large bowl, stir well with a whisk, cover and leave in a warm place for 1–2 hours or more time if it suits you. It won't rise much but you should see some bubbles as evidence of fermentation on the surface of the mix.

3. In the hour before you plan to do the final mix and bake, melt the butter and chocolate in a small heatproof bowl over a pan of simmering water. Set aside to cool for 30 minutes. Line a 25cm (10 in) square tin with baking parchment.

4. Preheat the oven to 160ºC/325ºF/gas mark 3.

5. Add the melted chocolate and butter plus the remaining stage 3 ingredients into the bowl with the batter. Whisk until well combined. Pour into the lined tin and smooth the top with the back of a spoon so it is evenly distributed.

6. Bake for 30-40 minutes until the top looks dry but it still has a slight wobble. It's difficult to overbake these. Sprinkle with additional sea salt, if liked, after they come out of the oven and leave to cool in the tin. When cool cut into squares to serve. The brownies can be stored in an airtight container for up to a week.

SAVOURY SOURDOUGH

FENNEL AND FETA MUFFINS

The electricity bill for the bakery is painfully high and so any residual heat from the oven that we can use after the bread has been baked feels like a win. I have fallen into the habit of using the deck oven for everything. I especially love to roast vegetables for salads, focaccia toppings and soups; it is also useful for fruit, compotes and jams. It preserves the best of the flavour and texture of vegetables. My roasting staples are olive oil, date syrup, salt and chilli, and also caraway when I think I can get away with it.

Savoury muffins are best with big flavours; there are many combinations that would work so use what you have to hand. Courgettes work well with feta and are a good choice when they are in season, or try spicy aubergine or red peppers with Taleggio or caramelised onions with Cheddar.

MAKES 12 MUFFINS

Stage 1: Refreshment
63g (2½ oz) strong white bread flour
95g (3¼ oz) whole milk
32g (1 oz) wheat starter at 60% hydration (12–24 hours after last refreshment)
16g (½ oz) caster sugar

For the roasted fennel
2–3 medium fennel bulbs, approximately 800g (1¾ lb)
2 tbsp olive oil
2 tbsp date syrup
½ tsp caraway seeds
large pinch of dried chilli flakes (optional)
salt

Stage 2: Batter mix
143g (5 oz) unsalted butter, chilled and cut into 2 cm (¾ in cubes)
194g (6¾ oz) white spelt flour
35g (1¼ oz) caster sugar
100g (3½ oz)/2 whole eggs, beaten
5g (⅛ oz) bicarbonate of soda
1g sea salt
200g (7 oz) feta, crumbled

1. Place all the stage 1 ingredients in a 1.5 litre (2¾ pint) jar or jug, cover and leave at room temperature for 4–6 hours.

2. Bring a large pan of salted water to the boil and preheat the oven to 200ºC/400ºF/gas mark 6. Fill a large bowl with cold water and line a baking tray with baking parchment.

3. Trim the base and stalks of the fennel bulbs, core and remove the woody outer layers and then thinly slice the green stalks. Slice the fennel bulbs, lengthways into segments about 7–8cm (2¾–3¼ in) long and 1cm (½ in) thick. Plunge the fennel segments and stalks, in batches, into the salted water for 1–2 minutes, remove and place in the cold water. Drain, dry on paper towels and place in a large bowl with a pinch of salt, the oil, date syrup, caraway seeds and chill flakes, if using. Toss to coat. Place on the lined tray and roast for 20–25 minutes, until the fennel is tender and caramelising on the outer edges. Once the fennel is cooked reduce the oven temperature to 180ºC/350ºF/gas mark 4.

4. Cut 12 x 10cm (4 in) squares of baking parchment and make a cut in each from one side to the centre of the square. Place a square of paper in each hole in the muffin tin, overlapping the centre cut edges, to form a rough cone shape. Alternatively, you can use paper muffin cases.

5. Place the butter, flour and sugar, for stage 2 in a freestanding mixer with paddle attachment or in a medium bowl. Mix on low speed or rub between your fingertips until the mixture resembles coarse breadcrumbs. Gently mix in the egg, bicarbonate of soda, salt and 190g of the starter, on low speed or with a spatula, until well combined. Fold in the feta and fennel. Divide the muffin mixture equally between the paper cones.

6. Bake the muffins immediately, or leave for 30–60 minutes until they are slightly risen. Bake for 20–25 minutes until they spring back when pressed lightly on top and a skewer inserted into the centre comes out clean. Leave the muffins to cool in the tin.

PUMPKIN SCONES

Growing up in Australia in the 1980s and 1990s, pumpkin scones were a familiar sight at birthday parties, school fêtes and bake sales alongside fairy bread, Anzac biscuits, lamingtons and the ubiquitous sausage sizzle. It was a good time and place to be a child! Most of these staples of my childhood result in blank stares from the British when I mention them and of all of them, it's the pumpkin scones which should be better known. I recall pumpkins as huge, dark green monsters that bore no resemblance to the Halloween versions shown on American TV shows. The tasty bright orange flesh had fantastic flavour and baked well, often appearing as part of a roast dinner. These scones don't taste of pumpkin, but it gives them a lovely tender texture that makes them very moreish.

MAKES 12 SCONES

Stage 1: Refreshment
102g (3½ oz) strong white bread flour
102g (3½ oz) whole milk
51g (2 oz) wheat starter at 60% hydration (12–24 hours after last refreshment)
25g (1 oz) caster sugar

For the roasted pumpkin
1kg (2¼ lb) pumpkin or butternut squash
15g (½ oz) olive oil

Stage 2 Dough mix
300g (11 oz) plain white flour
280g (10 oz) unsalted butter, chilled and cut into 2 cm (¾ in cubes)
75g (3 oz) caster sugar
6g (¼ oz) sea salt
13g (½ oz) baking powder

For the glaze
1 medium egg, beaten
2 tbsp Demerara sugar

1. Place all the stage 1 ingredients in a 1.5 litre (2¾ pint) jar or jug, mix and cover and leave in the fridge for 12–16 hours. Remove from the fridge and set aside for 2–4 hours at room temperature before mixing the dough. Alternatively, just leave at room temperature for 4–6 hours and don't chill.

2. Preheat the oven to 220ºC/425ºF/ gas mark 7. Remove the seeds from the pumpkin or squash and cut it into 10cm (4 in) chunks (there's no need to peel it). Place on a baking sheet lined with parchment and toss with the olive oil. Roast for 30 minutes or until tender. Allow to cool, peel the skin off and place in a bowl. Roughly mash and set aside.

3. Place the flour and butter for stage 2 in a free standing mixer with paddle attachment or in a medium bowl. Mix on low speed or rub between your fingertips until the mixture resembles coarse breadcrumbs. Add the sugar, salt and baking powder and stir with a spoon to distribute evenly. Add 275g (10 oz) of the starter and the mashed pumpkin and mix with a spoon until the dough comes together, then turn out onto the work surface and knead briefly and gently, until the dough is smooth and uniform in texture. Shape the dough into a 25cm (10 in) round, approximately 8–10cm (1 ½–2 in) thick, wrap in cling film and leave on the work surface for 1–2 hours then refrigerate for 1 hour or overnight.

4. Preheat the oven to 200ºC/400ºF/gas mark 6. Line a baking tray with baking parchment.

5. Unwrap the dough and place the round on the lined baking tray, cut it into quarters and then cut each quarter into 3. You should have 12 equal triangle wedges. Pull each wedge outwards a little, so there is a 1cm (½ in) gap between each piece but leaving them in the circle arrangement. Brush the wedges with egg and sprinkle with the Demerara sugar.

6. Bake for approximately 25–30 minutes until golden, top and bottom. Leave to cool on the tray until cool to the touch.

CHEESE SCONES

For the past few years I have eaten sourdough in pastry and in bread form more or less daily and have found my enjoyment of quick breads has diminished as I miss the depth and complexity that sourdough brings. This is true of most bread I eat in restaurants now too, even excellent bread can disappoint. I regret this sometimes, because perfectly delicious food no longer satisfies. We train our tastes with our choices and win and lose at times. Sourdough scones aren't more or less virtuous than any other kind of scone. They lack structure comparatively but gain flavour. I enjoy reinventing recipes and understanding their components; it's the process that is interesting and if the end result is delicious it is worth keeping alongside more traditional recipes.

MAKES 10–12 SCONES

Stage 1: Refreshment
131g (4½ oz) strong white bread flour
131g (4½ oz) whole milk
65g (2½ oz) wheat starter at 60% hydration (12–24 hours after last refreshment)
33g (1¼ oz) caster sugar

Stage 2: Dough mix
263g (9¼ oz) plain white flour
223g (7¾ oz) unsalted butter, chilled and cut into 2 cm (¾ in cubes)
61g (2½ oz) caster sugar
225g (8 oz) mature Cheddar, grated
1 tsp sea salt
10g (¼ oz) baking powder
½ tsp ground black pepper, English mustard powder or ground cayenne (optional)
60g (2½ oz) double cream, plus 1–2 tbsp for glazing

1. Place all the stage 1 ingredients in a 1.5 litre (2¾ pint) jar or jug, mix, cover and leave in the fridge for 12–16 hours. Remove from the fridge and set aside for 2–4 hours at room temperature, before mixing the dough. Alternatively just leave at room temperature for 4–6 hours and don't chill.

2. Place the flour and butter for stage 2 in a freestanding mixer with paddle attachment or in a medium bowl. Mix on low speed or rub between your fingertips until the mixture resembles coarse breadcrumbs. Add the sugar, 150g (5 oz) of the grated cheese, salt, baking powder and your chosen spice, if using. Stir with a spoon to distribute evenly. Add 354g (12¼ oz) of the starter and the cream and mix with a spoon until the dough comes together, then turn out onto the work surface and knead briefly and gently, until the dough is smooth and uniform in texture. Shape the dough into a 4–5cm (1 ½–2 in) thick and even round, wrap in cling film and leave on the work surface for 1–2 hours then refrigerate for 1 hour or overnight.

3. Preheat the oven to 200ºC/400ºF/gas mark 6. Line a baking tray with baking parchment.

4. Use a round cutter to cut circles out of the dough, placing them as close together as possible and using sharp, firm cuts – this helps the scones rise to their full height. You should get 10–12 scones from the dough. You can gently reroll the trimmings but they won't be quite so nice as those cut first.

5. Arrange the scones in rows about 1cm (½ in) apart, on the baking tray. Brush with cream and sprinkle with the remaining Cheddar. Bake until golden, top and bottom, and the cheese is bubbling – approximately 20–25 minutes. Leave the scones to cool on the tray or transfer to a wire wrack if you prefer.

SAVOURY SWIRLS

These swirls are a perfect example of how sweet and savoury flavours work well together. The rich, slightly sweet dough is as delicious with salty savoury fillings as it is with sweet Cinnamon Buns (see page 116). I actually prefer the savoury flavours and the Marmite and cheese filling is one of my favourites. Any of these fillings can also be used for the Babka (see page 112). The swirls work well for a crowd – you could make them half size and serve them warm as a savoury option for a children's birthday party; the adults will fall upon them at the very least.

MAKES 9 SWIRLS

1 x Brioche dough (complete the recipe on page 32 up until the dough goes into the fridge) flour, for dusting
1 x quantity filling of your choice (see below)

1. Line a 25cm (10 in) square cake tin with baking parchment.

2. On a lightly floured work surface, roll the chilled brioche dough into a 20 x 27cm (8 x 10¾ in) rectangle.

3. Spread the filling over the dough right to the edges on three sides but leaving a 1cm (½ in) border with no filling on one long side of the rectangle. Roll up the dough firmly from the long side with the filling on. Pinch the seam closed and arrange the roll so it is seam-side down on the work surface. Measure 3cm (1 in) increments along the roll and cut the dough into 9 with a sharp knife. Lay swirl side down, in the tin in 3 rows of 3.

4. Cover with a tea towel, making sure it does not touch the shaped dough, and allow it to rest for 16–24 hours in a warm place at around 24ºC (75ºF).

5. Twenty minutes before baking, preheat the oven to 200ºC/400ºF/gas mark 6 and place a 25cm (10 in) roasting tin inside.

6. Place the swirls in the oven and pour 150–200ml (5–7 fl oz) water into the roasting tin. Reduce the heat to 180ºC/350ºF/gas mark 4 and bake for 15 minutes then remove the roasting tin from the oven. Bake for a further 15–20 minutes or until the internal temp is 98ºC (208ºF) and a skewer inserted into the centre comes out clean (it may be sticky with the filling however). Serve warm or cold.

FILLINGS

MARMITE AND CHEDDAR

Chop 95g (3¼ oz) unsalted butter into small cubes, place in a bowl and set aside at room temperature, for 10–20 minutes, to soften. Add 95g (3¼ oz) Marmite to the butter and mix together until well combined. Spread the Marmite butter over the dough and sprinkle 200g (7 oz) grated mature Cheddar cheese on top.

PIZZA

Spread 200g (7 oz) pizza sauce (see page 149) over the dough and sprinkle 300g (11 oz) grated mozzarella cheese over. Top with the leaves from a small bunch of fresh basil.

CHEDDAR, DILL AND SPRING ONION

Chop 88g (3¼ oz) unsalted butter into small cubes, place in a bowl and set aside at room temperature for 10–20 minutes, to soften. Combine 26g (1 oz) grated mature Cheddar cheese, 21g finely chopped dill and 85g (3¼ oz) thickly-sliced spring onions. Spread the butter over the dough and sprinkle the cheese mixture on the top.

SOURDOUGH PIZZAS

Staff lunch at the bakery can be haphazard depending on the day and how much time there is so I increased the batches of pizza and focaccia dough so there is at least staff pizza if nothing else. It serves two purposes, one is to feed hungry and hard working staff and the other to allow experimentation with toppings and techniques without the pressure of it being presented to the customers. We take a relaxed approach so whoever has some time or an idea to test takes care of the topping and the baking. It is quite often the best and most delicious product to come out of the oven that day, so helps us improve our baking for customers. It's quite forgiving and utterly satisfying and even when imperfect in shape will be much better than most pizza you can buy.

**MAKES 3 LARGE OR
6 SMALL PIZZAS**
20cm (8 in) or 10cm (4 in)

Pizza bases
1 x Focaccia dough (complete
the recipe on page 35 up until
the dough goes into the fridge)
semolina, for sprinkling
sunflower oil, for greasing
flour, for dusting

Pizza sauce
350g (12 oz) passata
1 garlic clove, peeled and
squashed
1 tsp dried oregano
1 tsp sugar
½ tsp red wine vinegar
½ tsp salt;
2–3 tbsp extra virgin olive oil
dried chilli flakes or black
pepper, to taste

Pizza toppings
300g (11 oz) buffalo mozzarella,
torn into pieces
bunch of fresh basil

1. Three hours before you want to bake the pizza, remove the dough from the fridge and divide by weight into 3 or 6 portions. Shape into balls with lightly floured hands and a dough scraper and allow them to rest on the counter uncovered for 1–2 hours.

2. Combine all the ingredients for the sauce in a pan and simmer over a very low heat for at least 1 hour until reduced and thick. Check the seasoning and allow to cool before using.

3. Preheat the oven to 225ºC/425ºF/gas mark 7. Place 2 or 3 large baking trays (depending on the size of your oven) in the oven to preheat.

4. To prepare the bases, sprinkle semolina on a piece of baking parchment that will fit onto one of the baking trays. Carefully lift a ball of rested dough, turn it over so the side that was facing upwards is now touching the semolina. Using the semolina underneath to stop it from sticking, shape into a 20cm (8 in) round if you are making 3 pizzas or 10cm (4 in) round if you are making 6. Slightly oiled hands will prevent the dough sticking to your hands or you can very lightly flour the top of the pizza.

Try not to make any holes in the dough and leave the outer edges thicker than the centre of the pizza which should be quite thin. Try lifting the dough and shaping gently over the knuckles of your hand before placing it back down on to the semolina dusted paper. If the shape is not perfect or is more square than round, don't worry – they will still taste great.

5. Shape as many pizzas as you can bake in one go – it may be necessary to bake in batches. The others can be shaped while you wait for the first batch to bake.

6. Divide the tomato sauce between the pizzas and top with the torn mozzarella. Carefully lift or slide the pizzas, on the paper, onto the preheated trays.

7. Bake for 10–15 minutes. Check the bottom of the pizzas and if they are golden with dark brown edges and bubbling cheese then take them out. Allow to cool for a couple of minutes and then scatter torn basil leaves on top. Serve hot.

PUGLIESE POTATO FOCACCIA

I have a friend whom I have never met which is not uncommon in our ever-smaller world. Carla lives just outside Rome and once lived in London, running a restaurant in Bloomsbury long before I arrived here. Carla exudes knowledge, warmth and independence of mind and has been supportive of my experiments large and small from the start and continues to encourage me with each stage of the path I have taken these last few years. I first came across the idea of adding mashed potato to bread dough because Carla sent a book of hers to me. Carol Field's *The Italian Baker* is the kind of book one wishes one could write – well researched and written with warmth and substance. It is my first reference for all Italian bread questions and all the more special because it was in Carla's hands and kitchen before it was in mine.

MAKES 1 FOCACCIA
25cm (10in)

Stage 1: Refreshment
12g (½ oz) strong white bread flour
12g (½ oz) water
6g (¼ oz) whole wheat starter (8–12 hours after last refreshment)

Stage 2: Refreshment
20g (¾ oz) strong white bread flour
12g (½ oz) water
5g (¼ oz) caster sugar

Stage 3: Dough mix
120g (4 oz) potato, peeled and chopped into large pieces
354g (12¼ oz) strong white bread flour
283g (10 oz) water
4g (⅛ oz) sugar
8g (¼ oz) sea salt plus extra for sprinkling

For the toppings
150ml (5fl oz) olive oil, plus extra for greasing
300g (11 oz) large green olives, pitted
300g (11 oz) ripe baby plum tomatoes
small bunch of fresh oregano or 1 tsp dried oregano

1. Place all the stage 1 ingredients in a 300ml (10 fl oz) bowl or jar, mix, cover and leave at warm room temperature for 8–12 hours.

2. Add all the stage 2 ingredients to the bowl or jar containing the stage 1 starter, mix, cover and leave at warm room temperature for 8–10 hours.

3. Place the potato in a small pan of boiling water, simmer for 15–20 minutes or until soft. Drain and mash lightly, then set aside to cool.

4. Place all the remaining stage 3 ingredients, 88g (3¼ oz) the mashed potato and 42g (1½ oz) of the starter in a large bowl and mix with a spoon or your hand until no dry patches of flour remain visible, and then develop the dough in the bowl for 5–8 minutes. Or in a using the semolina underneath to stop it sticking while you shape, mix for 2 minutes on low speed and 3 minutes on a medium speed.

5. Use a little olive oil to lightly grease a rectangular flat bottomed glass or plastic container with a capacity of at least 3 litres (5¼ pints). Transfer the dough to the container, cover and rest for 30 minutes.

6. Fold the dough four times, leaving 30 minutes between each fold, then leave the dough for an additional hour to rest.

7. Cover and place in the fridge for a minimum of 16 hours or overnight.

8. Five hours before you want to serve the focaccia, line a 25cm (10 in) square or round baking tin with baking parchment. Brush the base of the tin with half the oil. Tip the cold dough into the tin, pour the remaining oil on top and leave it in a warm place for an hour or two.

9. With spread fingertips and using both hands, gently push into the dough. The goal at this stage is to gently and evenly take the dough to the edges of the tin after the gluten has had a chance to relax. It should bubble up around the indentations your fingers make.

10. Leave the dough for another 1–2 hours, scatter the olives, tomatoes and oregano over the dough and then repeat the fingertip process, pushing the olives and tomatoes into the dough. It should easily reach the edges of the tin at this stage but if it doesn't then wait a little longer. Repeat this process again if needed. The dough should have risen and have reached all sides of the tin with visible bubbles a light and pillowy appearance when it is ready to bake.

11. Twenty minutes before baking, preheat the oven to 240ºC/475ºF/gas mark 8. Place a metal roasting tin in the oven to preheat.

12. Sprinkle the dough with the fresh oregano leaves or dried oregano and a couple of pinches of sea salt and push into the dough, all over, one more time with your fingertips.

13. When you are ready to bake the focaccia, pour 100–200ml (3½–7 fl oz) water into the preheated metal tray and then load your focaccia into the oven. Reduce the heat to 225ºC/425ºF/gas mark 7. and bake for 30–35 minutes removing the roasting tray of water after 15–20 minutes. The focaccia is ready when the bottom of the loaf is golden.

14. Allow to cool for at least 30 minutes in the tin before cutting and serving. Store any leftover focaccia in a container at room temperature.

PESTO FLATBREADS

The year we opened one of our customers, Alex, presented me with bunches of wild garlic foraged in Dorset and I exchanged it for bread, a ritual we have repeated yearly ever since. Besides the wonderful flavour, wild garlic is robust and so retains its shape and colour when baked in bread or on pastry. I recommend adding it to any of the plain breads you find in this book or using it to top focaccia. These flatbreads are inspired by Olia Hercules' Moldovan breads made with kefir dough and sorrel from her wonderful book *Mamushka*. When wild garlic is not in season, use any mix of bold green herbs and leaves. The flatbreads are wonderful with feta too as in the original version or with a scattering of torn mozzarella over the pesto before you seal the parcel up.

MAKES 15 FLATBREADS

Stage 1: Refreshment
42g (1½ oz) strong white bread flour
42g (1½ oz) whole milk
21g (¾ oz) wheat starter at 60% hydration (12–16 hours after last refreshment)

Stage 2: Refreshment
200g (7 oz) white flour
300g (11 oz) whole milk
50g (2 oz) caster sugar

For the pesto
200g (7 oz) wild garlic or a mix of basil, rocket and mint leaves and ½ bulb of garlic, cloves peeled
1 small hot chilli or a large pinch of dried chilli flakes
2 pinches of salt
1 tsp sugar
zest of ⅛ of a lemon
3–4 tbsp olive oil

Stage 3: Dough mix
555g (1¼ lb) white bread flour
11g (¼ oz) caster sugar
5g (⅛ oz) sea salt
8g (¼ oz) bicarbonate of soda
100g (3½ oz) sunflower oil plus extra for greasing

1. Place all the stage 1 ingredients in a 1.5 litre (2¾ pint) jar or jug, mix, cover and leave at room temperature for 10–16 hours.

2. Add all the stage 2 ingredients to the jar or jug containing the stage 1 starter, cover and leave at warm room temperature for 4–6 hours.

3. For the pesto, blend all the ingredients together in a small food processor. Or finely chop the wild garlic or herbs and garlic and combine with the remaining pesto ingredients in a medium bowl. Taste for seasoning and adjust as needed. Set aside.

4. Place the flour, sugar, salt and bicarbonate of soda for stage 3 and 400g (14 oz) of starter in the bowl of a free standing mixer fitted with a dough hook. Mix until the dough is smooth and shiny, around 5–6 minutes. Alternatively, mix the flour, sugar, salt and bicarbonate of soda for stage 3 and 400g (14 oz) of starter in a bowl and then turn out onto the work surface and knead for 8–10 minutes until you have a pliable, stretchy dough.

5. Place in an oiled bowl, cover and leave at room temperature for 30–60 minutes.

6. Divide your dough into 15 x 40g (1½ oz) pieces and place on a lightly oiled work surface to rest.

7. Heat a medium sized non-stick frying pan until hot and pour 1 tbsp of sunflower oil into the pan just before you are ready to start frying.

8. Oil the work surface and your hands and flatten a piece of dough with the palm of your hand on the work surface and begin stretching its edges out, pinning the edges to the work surface to hold them as you work around the piece of dough, forming it into a round shape. When you can't make it any thinner without tearing, spread a heaped tablespoon of pesto on one half of the dough, leaving the edges clear of filling and fold the other half over the half with the filling. Pinch the edges of the dough together, to seal.

9. One at a time, carefully lift the flatbreads into the hot frying pan. Fry on one side, over a medium heat, for 2–3 minutes until golden, then flip the flatbread and fry on the other side for 1–2 minutes. Repeat to cook the remaining flatbreads, wiping the pan clean and adding 1 tbsp of oil before frying each flatbread. Eat hot.

SMOKED CHEESE AND BEETROOT
PULL APART BREAD

I gave up bacon many years ago and with time I realised that it was the smoky flavour that was the main appeal of bacon and smoked cheese is a great substitute for when you need a punchy flavour. One of my favourite sandwiches to make is a latke with smoked cheese and red cabbage slaw in our New York Light Rye bread (see page 28); it's the best sandwich in the world. This recipe is along the same lines with smoked cheese and sweet, slightly spicy beetroot relish. The components get assembled as a vertical sandwich and so can be torn apart by pulling segments from the ends.

MAKES 1 LOAF

500g (1 lb 2 oz) (half quantity) Sourdough Laminated Pastry Dough (see pages 80–81)

For the filling
150g (5 oz) smoked Cheddar, grated
pinch of salt
freshly ground black pepper
150g (5 oz) Beetroot and Caraway jam (see page 208)

1. Line a 500g (1 lb 2 oz) loaf tin with baking parchment to 3–4cm (1¼–1½ in) above the height of the tin.

2. Roll the dough into a rectangle approximately 18 x 40cm (7 x 16 in) and trim all four edges – they don't have to be perfectly straight. Spread a layer of beetroot jam over the dough and sprinkle over the grated Cheddar, in an even layer.

3. Measure and cut the dough into 12 equal smaller rectangles, approximately 6 x 10cm (2½ x 4 in). Make four stacks of three pieces, placed one on top of the other. From the bottom each stack will be dough, filling, dough, filling, dough, filling. Next place each of the four stacks on top of each other, repeating the pattern. Turn the final top square over, so you have dough, not filling at the top of the stack.

4. Place the stack vertically into the lined tin, like a sandwich that has been stood up on its side. There should be some space between the layers because as they proof the pastry layers should expand outwards to fill the gaps, but they should stand stable in the tin and support each other. Proof for 20–24 hours at 24ºC (75ºF).

5. Twenty minutes before baking, preheat the oven to 220ºC/425ºF/gas mark 7 and place a metal roasting tin in the oven. Pour 100–200ml (3½–7 fl oz) water into the preheated metal tray and place the bread in the oven. Bake for 15 minutes, then remove the tray of water and bake for additional 20–25min until the internal temp is 98ºC (208ºF) and a skewer inserted into the centre comes out clean. The pull apart bread should be golden brown on the sides and on top.

SAVOURY SOURDOUGH

ONION FOCACCIA TARTE TATIN

Mattie Taiano is a young chef who often pops into the bakery and when he does, we discuss food. He told me about an onion bread which he had come across; a thick slab of focaccia covered in onions on every side and I couldn't rest until I had tried it. I make a huge tray – flipping 3kg (6 lb 10 oz) of dough in a tin that has come out of a 275ºC (527ºF) oven is invigorating to say the least, there's an excellent chance it could hit the floor or burn my arm but so far, so good. Any time there is a large amount of onions in the oven the smell permeates everything, but smelling of fried onions is a fair price to present this on the counter – it's utterly delicious.

MAKES 1 FOCACCIA
1kg (2¼ lb)

Stage 1: Refreshment
10g (¼ oz) water
10g (¼ oz) strong white bread flour
5g (⅛ oz) wheat starter (8–12 hours after its last refreshment)

Stage 2: Refreshment
33g (1¼ oz) strong white bread flour
20g (¾ oz) water
8g (¼ oz) caster sugar

Stage 3: Dough mix
525g (1 lb 2½ oz) strong white bread flour
369g (12½ oz) water
65g (2½ oz) extra virgin olive oil
11g (¼ oz) sea salt plus extra for seasoning
7g (¼ oz) caster sugar

For the onions
250ml 8fl oz extra virgin olive oil plus extra for greasing
1kg (2¼ lb) red onions, peeled and very thinly sliced into half moons.

1. Mix all the stage 1 ingredients in a jar or container with a lid, with a capacity of at least 500ml (17fl oz). Cover and leave at room temperature for 8–12 hours.

2. Mix all the stage 2 ingredients into the jar or container containing the stage 1 starter, cover and leave at warm room temperature for 8–10 hours.

3. Combine the ingredients for stage 3 in a large bowl with 63g (2½ oz) of the starter. Mix with a spoon or your hand until no dry patches of flour remain visible and then mix in the bowl for 5–8 minutes. Or, in a freestanding mixer with dough hook attached, mix for 2 minutes to combine ingredients and then 3 minutes on medium speed. The gluten won't fully develop at this stage and it won't be completely smooth, it will continue to develop with the folds.

4. Use a little olive oil to grease a large mixing bowl or a rectangular flat bottomed glass or plastic container with a capacity of at least 3 litres (5¼ pints). Transfer the dough to the bowl or container, cover and rest for 30 minutes.

5. Fold the dough four times, leaving 30 minutes between each fold, then give the dough an additional hour to rest.

6. Place in the fridge for a minimum of 16 hours or for up to 5 days.

7. Five hours before you want to bake the focaccia, line a 25cm (10 in) square baking tin with baking parchment. Brush over half the olive oil. Sprinkle half the onions in the bottom of the tin and season.

8. Tip the cold dough into the tin, rub a little oil on top and leave it in a warm place for 1–2 hours.

9. With spread fingertips and using both hands gently push the dough in straight lines following the lines of the tin. It is easiest if your hands are slightly damp or slightly oiled. The goal at this stage is to gently and evenly take the dough to the edges of the tin after the gluten has had a chance to relax.

10. Leave the dough for another hour and then repeat the fingertip stretching process. It should easily reach the edges of the tin at this stage but if it doesn't then wait a little longer. Repeat this process again if needed. The dough is ready to bake when it has risen and reached all sides of the tin and there are visible bubbles and it has a light and pillowy appearance. Scatter the remaining onions over the top of the dough, push them lightly into the dough and pour the remaining olive oil on top and season with salt.

continued overleaf

11. Give the dough another hour before baking but don't push the dough again – for this recipe you are looking for a slab of dough coated in onions rather than a dimpled focaccia.

12. Twenty minutes before baking preheat the oven to 225°C/435°F/gas mark 7. Place a metal roasting tin in the oven to preheat.

13. When you are ready to bake, pour 100–200ml (3½–7fl oz) water into the preheated metal tray and bake the focaccia for 20 minutes. Then, remove the roasting tin from the oven, take the focaccia out and quickly and carefully flip it over onto a piece of baking parchment then, and slide it back into the baking tin. The onion-coated underside will now be at the top of the tin. Reduce the oven temperature to 200°C/400°F/gas mark 6 and bake for another 15 minutes. Check the base of the focaccia – when it's golden and the onions are caramelised then it's ready.

14. Allow to cool for at least 30 minutes in the tin before cutting and serving. Store any leftovers at room temperature.

AUBERGINE EINKORN GALETTES

When I developed this recipe, I wanted to make a wholegrain pastry that was tasty but soft, not dry and crumbly. The sourdough increases the pastry's tenderness as well as increasing the availability of the nutrients in the wholegrains. It works well with sweet fillings too; I have made a jam tart with it, similar to a crostata which was lovely. The aubergine filling is based on vegetarian fillings for borekas; Claudia Roden's *The Book of Jewish Food* is always my first point of reference for Middle Eastern cooking and this resembles a caponata so falls somewhere between Sicily and the Middle East. I'm not given to a purist approach to cooking, I sometimes wish I could be more single minded in my preferences and style, but I go in all directions and don't feel badly about it at all.

**MAKES 6 SMALL OR
1 LARGE GALETTE**

For the filling
3 medium aubergines, sliced into 2 x 8cm (¾ x 3¼ in) pieces
olive oil, for drizzling
1 small red onion, finely chopped
4 garlic cloves, peeled and crushed
40g (1½ oz) pine nuts
3 ripe plum tomatoes, deseeded and roughly chopped, or 200g (7 oz) passata
1–2 pinches dried chilli flakes, or to taste
40g (1½ oz) currants or raisins
1–2 tbsp date syrup
1 tbsp salted capers, rinsed and roughly chopped
½ tsp paprika
1–2 tsp red wine vinegar
1 small bunch fresh mint, leaves only, finely chopped
1 small bunch fresh coriander, roughly chopped
sea salt and freshly ground black pepper

continued overleaf

1. Preheat the oven to 220ºC/425ºF/gas mark 7. Line a baking tray with baking parchment

2. For the filling, place the aubergines in a single layer on the lined tray. Drizzle with olive oil and season. Bake for 20–25 minutes, turning occasionally, until golden and tender.

3. While the aubergines bake, heat the remaining olive oil in a large saucepan and fry the onion with a pinch of salt for 10 minutes until soft and slightly caramelised. Add the garlic and pine nuts and cook for 3–4 minutes until they take on some colour but take care not to burn them. Add the tomatoes or passata, chilli, currants or raisins and date syrup to the onions with a little more salt and simmer for 10–15 minutes over low heat. When the aubergines are baked, add them to the pan and simmer for another 20–30 minutes. Add a little water if the mix is too dry. The idea is to cook it down to a paste rather than end up with a wet sauce. For the last 5 minutes add the capers and paprika. Remove from the heat and stir in the vinegar. Taste for seasoning and adjust as needed – you are looking for a balance of sweet, sour, spicy and salty. Add more vinegar, salt or paprika if needed.

4. Set aside to cool until almost at room temperature and add the chopped herbs. Leave for 30 minutes, taste again for seasoning and adjust as needed. Set aside.

5. For the pastry, place the flour and butter in a freestanding mixer fitted with paddle attachment or in a medium bowl. Mix on low speed or rub between your fingertips until the mixture resembles coarse breadcrumbs.

6. Mix the starter with the water in a small bowl and add to the flour and butter mix with the salt and the yoghurt. Stir with a butter knife until it comes together as a dough and then knead briefly until the dough comes together as a uniform, smooth ball. Form into a fat disc and wrap in clingfilm. Leave somewhere warm for 2 hours so the dough can ferment and then refrigerate for at least 1 hour or up to 2 days.

7. Remove the pastry from the fridge 20–30 minutes before you want to assemble the tarts. Preheat the oven to 180ºC/350ºF/gas mark 4.

continued overleaf

For the pastry

254g (9 oz) wholemeal einkorn flour plus extra for dusting

182g (6½ oz) unsalted butter, chilled and cut into 2 cm (¾ in cubes)

25g (1 oz) wheat starter (12–16 hours since its last refreshment)

38g (1½ oz) water

97g (3½ oz) full fat Greek yogurt

4g (⅛ oz) sea salt

For assembling

1 medium egg, lightly beaten

30g (1 oz) nigella seeds (optional)

8. Roll the pastry out as thinly as you can on a lightly floured surface. Cut out 6 circles approximately 15cm (6 in) in diameter, rerolling the pastry if necessary. Alternatively roll a single 30cm (12 in) circle of pastry, turning the pastry by a quarter with each roll so it is even and round.

9. Place the ring(s) on a baking tray and line them with baking parchment. Place the pastry in the ring(s) – there should be 2.5–5cm (1–2 in) of pastry hanging over the edge. Spread the filling over the base and fold the excess pastry towards the middle. Brush the edges of the galettes with beaten egg and sprinkle with nigella seeds, if using.

10. Bake for 20–25 minutes or until the pastry is golden top and bottom and the filling hot. Use the paper to lift the galettes out of the rings or the tins. Serve hot, warm or cold.

MARGOT
SPECIALITIES

LILY'S TAHINI COOKIES

On a trip to Jerusalem, many years ago, we stayed with family friends and ate these cookies for breakfast with coffee, while overlooking the city. Our host, Lily, generously translated the recipe from Hebrew to English for me and I scribbled it on a scrap of paper. I have never found a recipe I like better than this one, the cookies are crumbly, delicious and perfect. We make the same recipe in the bakery, but with peanut butter replacing tahini, as the peanut butter version is more popular with customers but I rejoice when the peanut butter runs low and I can squeeze in a batch using tahini.

MAKES 20 COOKIES

140g (4½ oz) unsalted butter, at room temperature
140g (4½ oz) caster sugar
180g (6¼ oz) tahini or unsalted smooth peanut butter
255g (9 oz) plain flour
5g (⅛ oz) baking powder
5g (⅛ oz) sea salt
20 (¾ oz) whole almonds, blanched (optional)

1. Preheat the oven to 160°C/325ºF/gas mark 3. Line a baking tray with baking parchment

2. Cream the butter and sugar together in a free standing mixer or in a bowl with a handheld electric mixer for 2–3 minutes until well combined but not too creamy, or the biscuits will spread too much when baked.

3. Add the tahini or peanut butter and mix briefly, then fold in the flour, baking powder and sea salt on a low speed or using a spatula, until the dough is uniform and comes together.

4. Divide the dough into 12 x 35g (1¼ oz) pieces and roll each piece into a ball. Push your thumb into the centre of the ball to flatten it slightly and leave an indent. Push a whole almond, if using, into the indent. Space the cookies evenly on the tray – they do spread during baking.

5. Bake for 15 minutes then turn the tray and bake for another 10–15 minutes. They should be lightly browned on the underside (lift one very carefully to check) and should have a golden colour on top. It's better to slightly over, rather than under, bake these for the best texture and flavour.

EDIBLE FLOWER SHORTBREADS

Before I opened Margot I ran a cake business; it coincided with the early days of the cupcake trend and at a time when blogs were a key method of communication with other bakers. I decorated in royal icing – from princesses and cartoon characters to logos – anything a customer asked for. When I came to open Margot I wanted a new approach to decoration and though we still write 'happy birthday' on cakes or decorate cookies, we work in a more natural style. The universe gives us flowers far more beautiful than any that can be formed by even the most practiced hand and it has never been easier to source flowers suitable for baking. Here, the biscuits are baked slowly and gently so that the flowers retain as much colour as possible.

MAKES 20 BISCUITS

295g (10½ oz) plain flour plus extra for rolling
110g (3¾ oz) icing sugar
¼ tsp sea salt
195g (6¾ oz) unsalted butter, chilled and cut into
2cm (¾ in) cubes
40g (1½ oz)/2 egg yolks

Flavourings
Choose 1 of the following:
½ vanilla pod, split and scraped
1 tbsp dried lavender flowers and finely grated zest of half a lemon or an orange
½ tsp crushed fennel seeds
1 lemon or orange, zested

To finish
100g (3½ oz) caster sugar
30 edible flowers and leaves

1. Place the flour, icing sugar and salt in a medium bowl. Add the butter and rub in with your fingertips until the mixture resembles coarse breadcrumbs. Don't over mix at this stage. Add the egg yolks and your choice of the four flavourings and mix briefly until the dough comes together in a uniform ball.

2. Form the dough into a fat disc, wrap in clingfilm and chill for 30–60 minutes. You can chill for longer, even overnight, but the dough will need some time to soften before rolling.

3. Place the caster sugar in a bowl. Line a baking tray with baking parchment.

4. Briefly knead the dough again on an unfloured work surface until it is smooth but still cold.

5. On a lightly floured surface, roll out the dough. Roll away from yourself from the centre of the piece outward, and turn the dough with a quarter turn with each roll. This will prevent the dough crumbling and breaking or getting stuck to the surface. Work quickly as you roll, as the dough needs to be cool to get the best shape for the biscuits.

6. When the dough is about 1cm (½ in) thick, lay the edible flowers over the dough – you can be as precise or as free as you wish with their placing. Continue rolling until the dough is about 5mm (¼ in) thick, pushing the flowers into the surface of the dough as you roll.

7. Cut out the biscuits using a 5cm (2½ in) cutter. Dip each biscuit in the caster sugar to coat both sides. Place on the lined tray. The dough scraps can be rerolled once, to cut out more biscuits. Chill on the tray for at least 30 minutes before baking.

8. Preheat the oven to 160°C/325°F/gas mark 3.

9. Bake the shortbreads for 20–25 minutes, turning the tray after 15 minutes. The shortbreads won't colour much – they are ready when lightly golden on the underside and the top edges of each biscuit has some colour. Cool on the tray.

BUYING AND PREPARING EDIBLE FLOWERS

I buy fresh edible flowers for the bakery online from Maddocks Farm Organics in Devon – they really are very special.

Smaller flowers need no preparation for the shortbread biscuits. For larger flowers, remove the petals from their thicker bases so they can be easily pressed into the dough.

GINGERBREAD DINOSAURS

I often joke that if we stopped making these cookies, the children of East Finchley would riot. We sometimes run out of bread and occasionally sell out of pastries, but one of the core principles of managing the pastry section and front of house at Margot is that gingerbread dinosaurs must be on the counter at all times.

In 2006 I saw a picture of an extraordinary small, pink and white striped cake made by cake designer Peggy Porschen. I started to contemplate a baking career and I was offered a job working with a talented baker and designer. Janine had worked with Peggy at Konditor and Cook, where I later went on to train. This recipe is based on Peggy's gingerbread – they hold their shape beautifully, taste wonderful and keep well. The dough takes several hours to prepare and for best results can be made 1–2 days before baking.

MAKES 15 BISCUITS

For the gingerbread
60g (2½ oz) golden syrup
18g (½ oz) orange juice
1 tsp ground cinnamon
1 tsp ground ginger
90g (3¼ oz) dark brown sugar
100g (3½ oz) unsalted butter, roughly cubed
½ tsp bicarbonate of soda
225g (8 oz) plain flour, sifted, plus extra for dusting
pinch of salt

For the royal icing (optional)
250g (9 oz) icing sugar
40g (1½ oz)/1 egg white
squeeze of lemon juice
paste food colours (optional)

1. Place the syrup, orange juice, spices and sugar in a medium saucepan. Heat over a low heat until the sugar has dissolved and then bring to the boil. Remove from the heat and stir in the butter until melted, then mix in the bicarbonate of soda. Leave to cool in the pan for 30 minutes and then transfer to a freestanding mixer fitted with paddle attachment or medium bowl. With the mixer or a wooden spoon, stir in the flour and salt, until smooth. Don't over mix.

2. Form the dough into two flat discs, wrap and chill in the fridge, until firm, for at least an hour or up to 2 days.

3. Line two baking trays with parchment.

4. Remove the dough from fridge and if it is very firm re-knead a couple of times on a work surface so the dough is still cold but pliable enough to roll.

5. On a lightly floured surface, roll out the first disc of dough until it is 3–5mm (⅛–¼ in) thick. Roll away from yourself from the centre of the piece outward, and turn the dough with a quarter turn with each roll. This will avoid the dough crumbling and breaking or getting stuck to the surface. Use minimal flour so when you re-roll the dough it won't be too dry.

6. Cut out shapes with the cutter and lay them on the tray, well spaced out as they will expand when baking. Roll your second disc and then combine the trimmings and roll once or twice more.

7. Chill the cookie shapes again for 30–60 minutes before baking.

8. When you are ready to bake preheat the oven to 180ºC/350ºF/gas mark 4.

9. Bake the biscuits for 18–25 minutes, turning the tray once during baking. They are ready when they have darkened in colour evenly across the top of the biscuit and look slightly dry. They keep baking on the hot trays after they come out of the oven so try and take them out a minute or two before they are quite done.

10. Leave the biscuits to cool on the tray – they will harden as they cool. Once cool, store in an airtight container or decorate with royal icing.

11. To make the icing, place one third of the icing sugar in a small bowl with the egg white and a few drops of lemon juice. Mix with a handheld electric mixer until smooth then add the remaining icing sugar and continue mixing for 2–3 minutes. If it looks dry and crumbly around the edges, add a drop or two

more lemon juice. The icing should hold its shape in soft peaks and have a smooth, glossy appearance when it is ready. If it has too many air bubbles from over mixing or is too stiff, it will be difficult to work with. If it is too dry lemon juice can be added at any point.

12. If you are not going to use the icing straight away, place it in a covered container immediately or the icing will dry out. Mix paste food colours into the icing, if using, and fill the piping bag(s) with royal icing. Cut a small hole in the piping bag(s) and pipe designs on your cookies. Start with a dot to secure the icing to the cookie, allow a line of icing to fall on the cookie, directed by your piping bag using even pressure from your thumb at the top of the bag and your free hand to guide the tip. Finish with a dot to anchor it when you have piped the line. Leave the icing to dry for several hours before storing the biscuits in an airtight container.

MARGOT SPECIALITIES

SALTED CARAMEL CHOCOLATE CHIP COOKIES

The appeal of these cookies is that they can be made on a quiet day, stored in the fridge and baked fresh daily with an improvement in taste and texture with each day (up to five or so). They also have a high chocolate to dough ratio; it's disappointing to eat a chocolate chip cookie with too little chocolate and I recommend using your favourite eating chocolate. Inspired by the famous *New York Times* chocolate chip cookie recipe, they use bread flour and we often prep extra salted caramel too: make the recipe below and you will have more than enough. The caramel is great to drizzle over the cookies or an apple cake, fold into buttercream and for pouring over ice cream, so I recommend doubling the recipe if you're a caramel fan.

MAKES 12 COOKIES

For the salted caramel
100g (3½ oz) water
235g (8¼ oz) caster sugar
170g (6 oz) double cream
sea salt, to taste

For the cookie dough
50g (2 oz) unsalted butter, at room temperature
54g (2 oz) tahini or smooth peanut butter
92g (3¼ oz) caster sugar
92g (3¼ oz) dark brown sugar
½ tsp vanilla extract
50g (2 oz)/1 whole egg, lightly beaten
108g (3¾ oz) plain flour
108g (3¾ oz) strong white bread flour
8g (¼ oz) baking powder
¼ tsp sea salt
150g (5 oz) dark chocolate, at least 66% cocoa solids, roughly chopped
50g (2 oz) toasted sesame seeds or chopped roasted peanuts, for sprinkling (optional)
sea salt, for sprinkling (optional)

1. First make the salted caramel – it can be prepared the day before baking or earlier on the day of baking. Place the water and sugar in a medium saucepan, cover and heat over a low heat until the sugar dissolves and the liquid is clear. Stir regularly and keep the lid on the pan as this will stop sugar crystals forming around the edges, which will affect the caramel.

2. When the sugar has dissolved, increase the heat and bring to the boil, but do not stir. When the caramel begins to turn dark brown, after 5–10 minutes, swirl the sugar mix in the pan a few times and then remove from the heat.

3. Quickly and carefully add the cream and stir in with a whisk – it will spit and bubble. Stir over a low heat until smooth, for another minute or so. The darker the caramel the stronger the flavour and the firmer the set will be, but don't over heat it or the caramel will be bitter. Add salt to taste whilst the caramel is warm. Allow to cool and store in the fridge until needed or for up to one week.

4. To make the cookies, place the butter, tahini or peanut butter, sugars and vanilla in a medium bowl and mix with an electric mixer or a spatula until slightly pale. Don't overmix or the cookies will spread too much on baking. Add the egg, in two additions, beating in well. Add the both of the flours, baking powder and salt and fold in. Just before it is fully mixed stir in the chocolate.

5. Divide the dough into 12 x 60g (2½ oz) balls. Chill for a minimum of 2 hours or for up to 5 days and bake from cold.

6. When you are ready to bake, preheat the oven to 160°C/ 325°F/gas mark 3.

7. Arrange balls of cookie dough in evenly spaced rows on a large baking tray lined with parchment. Bake for 15–18 minutes until golden around the edges and still soft in the centre. Use a spoon to drizzle with cold caramel, as they come out of the oven, and sprinkle with toasted sesame seeds, peanuts or a pinch of sea salt, if desired. Leave to cool on the tray.

BANANA SPELT MUFFINS

When I decided to add muffins to our repertoire, they seemed a logical extension of our morning offering – a little more fruit and a little less sugar and butter than cakes and pastries. I was aiming for tender muffins as good in the afternoon or even the next day as they are just after baking, and that did not dry out as soon as they cooled down. We make various flavours at the bakery but the banana muffin remains the customers' favourite and a favourite for the bakers too, who are at their busiest in the hour before the shop opens. A banana is quick to peel and mash compared to chopping apple or grating carrot! They sell well all year round and take minimal time to make. The dry mix and wet mix can be prepared the day before and then refrigerated separately, so they can be quickly baked in the morning for breakfast.

MAKES 12 MUFFINS

408g (14½ oz) white spelt flour
174g (6 oz) caster sugar
½ tsp sea salt
10g (¼ oz) baking powder
204g (7¼ oz) unsalted butter, chilled and cut into 2cm (¾ in) cubes
145g (5 oz)/3 whole eggs, lightly beaten
105g (3¾ oz) whole milk
400g (14 oz) mashed banana (3-4 small to medium bananas)
50g (2 oz) Demerara sugar

1. Preheat the oven to 180ºC/350ºF/gas mark 4. Line a muffin tin with paper cases or cut 12 x 10cm (4 in) squares of baking parchment and make a cut in each from one side to the centre of the square. Place a square of paper in each hole in the muffin tin, overlapping the centre cut edges, to form a rough cone shape.

2. Place the flour, caster sugar, salt, baking powder and butter in a medium bowl or in a freestanding mixer fitted with paddle attachment. Rub between your fingertips or mix on low speed until the mixture resembles coarse breadcrumbs.

3. Add the eggs and milk and mix briefly. Add the banana and fold through using a spatula.

4. Divide the mixture equally between the paper cases, approximately 120g (4 oz) per muffin. Sprinkle the Demerara over the top and bake immediately for 25-30 minutes until a skewer comes out clean, or the sponge bounces back when lightly pressed. Cool in the tin.

TRY A DIFFERENT FLAVOUR

The basic recipe for these muffins can easily be adapted - instead of the banana add an extra 30g (1 oz) of milk plus the following:

- **Berry:** 400g (14 oz) fresh or frozen blueberries or blackberries.
- **Blackberry and apple:** 200g (7 oz) blackberries and 200g (7 oz) skin-on apple, finely cubed.
- **Apple and cinnamon:** 400g (14 oz) skin-on eating apple, finely cubed and 12g (½ oz) ground cinnamon.
- **Carrot:** 400g (14 oz) grated carrot, 6g (¼ oz) ground ginger and 6g (¼ oz) ground cinnamon

SPELT HONEY CAKES

Honey cake is traditionally made and served for Rosh Hashanah, the Jewish New Year, and symbolises hope for a sweet year ahead. One Passover the conversation turned to honey cake and a fellow guest, Karen, gave me the first incarnation of this recipe. It was originally made with only golden syrup, but for the bakery I decided it ought to follow tradition. That first year when the planning and baking for pretty much all festivals and events happened a matter of days before, there was very little time to rest the cakes. A trial with spelt flour made a tender cake that could be eaten on the day of baking or kept for several weeks; ageing honey cakes is fairly traditional and some can only be enjoyed after maturing for at least a week. Marta and I worked on this recipe until it tookits current form and it hasn't changed since.

MAKES 2 LOAVES
1.25kg (2¾ lb)

467g (1lb ½ oz) white
spelt flour
350g (12 oz) caster sugar
24g (¾ oz) baking powder
16g (½ oz) ground cinnamon
373g (13 oz) water
280g (10 oz)/6 whole eggs,
lightly beaten
346g (12 oz) sunflower oil
272g (9½ oz) honey
272g (9½ oz) golden syrup

1. Preheat the oven to 160ºC/325ºF/gas mark 3. Line 2 x loaf tins with baking parchment.

2. Place the flour, sugar, baking powder, cinnamon and water in a large bowl or a freestanding mixer fitted with paddle attachment. Stir until just mixed then gradually add the eggs, whisking constantly or with the mixer running, until well combined. Add the oil in a slow, steady stream and finally add the honey and golden syrup and stir until completely mixed.

3. Divide the mixture equally between the lined tins and bake for 40–50 minutes or until a skewer inserted into the centre comes out clean. Don't open the oven for the first 40 minutes to avoid the cakes collapsing.

4. Remove the cakes from the oven and set aside to cool in the tins. Once cold, remove the baking parchment and wrap well in cling film. The cakes will keep for 2–3 weeks in a cool place.

SPELT HONEY CAKES

HAZELNUT FRIANDS

It's always a good idea to have recipes that use egg whites in a bakery where egg yolks are used alone in many recipes. If we make panettone or custard or pastry and have excess whites, we make these cakes. Based on the French financier, which is smaller and more delicate, these are an Australian café staple. The flavour of the nuts shines through; undimmed by other rich ingredients that would temper their flavour in another style of cake. They can be made in multiple flavours; citrus and berries often feature and they are quick to put together. Drizzle these with some chocolate glaze (see Chocolate Cake with Chocolate Glaze, page 186) and they are elegant enough for a dessert. You can use a friand tin or muffin tin but they also bake well as individual mini cakes or as a single, large thin torte.

**MAKES 1 LARGE OR
9–12 INDIVIDUAL CAKES**

For the sponge
250g (9 oz) unsalted butter
¼ vanilla pod, split and scraped
270g (9½ oz) icing sugar
80g (3 oz) plain white flour
plus extra for dusting
140g (4½ oz) hazelnuts,
toasted and ground
30g (1 oz) dark chocolate,
finely chopped
225g (8 oz)/5½ egg whites
pinch of salt

1. Preheat the oven to 190ºC/375ºF/gas mark 5. Grease and flour a 25cm (10 in) tin for a large cake or use pastry rings for individual sponges.

2. Place the butter and vanilla seeds in small pan and heat gently until the butter has melted. Strain through a sieve and set aside.

3. Place the icing sugar, flour, ground hazelnuts and chocolate in a medium bowl and stir with a whisk to combine

4. Place the eggs whites and salt in a medium bowl and lightly whisk together. Whisk the egg whites into the icing sugar mixture until fully combined. Then whisk in the melted butter until it is fully absorbed. Do not over mix.

5. Divide the mixture equally, by weight, into your prepared tin or rings.

6. Place in the oven, and reduce the oven temperature to 160°C/325ºF/gas mark 3. Bake for 20–25 minutes until the friands spring back when lightly pressed in the centre and a skewer inserted into the centre comes out clean.

7. Leave to cool in the tin or rings for 10 minutes then turn out of the tin with a firm tap while still warm. Once they have cooled, store in an airtight container for up to 3 days.

MARGOT SPECIALITIES

FIG KHORASAN CAKE

This cake works equally well with plums or dark berries, though I include figs as they have a geographical connection that pleases me; khorasan being an ancient variety of wheat originating in the region that is now modern Iran and Afghanistan. I make it when I want a simple fruity cake for the counter or at home. The khorasan flour works well with the rich fruit, it is a flour with an interesting, nutty flavour and is nutrient-rich. There is some evidence that it is easier to tolerate and digest for those who don't feel well eating the modern varieties of wheat and can have a beneficial impact on health – not often a claim made about cake. I don't substitute ingredients in baking such as sugar, eggs or dairy unless the end result is better for the change and here, it is.

MAKES 1 CAKE
20cm (8 in)

126g (4½ oz) unsalted butter, at room temperature
183g (6½ oz) caster sugar
½ tsp vanilla extract
115g (4 oz)/2½ whole eggs, lightly beaten
218g (7¾ oz) khorasan flour
6g (¼ oz) baking powder
½ tsp sea salt
20–30g (¾–1 oz) whole milk
350g (12 oz) figs, stalks removed and cut into thick slices
50g (2 oz) Demerara sugar

1. Preheat the oven to 160°C/325ºF/gas mark 3. Grease and line a 20cm (8 in) round cake tin with baking parchment.

2. Place the butter and sugar in a medium bowl or a mixer with paddle attachment. Beat with a spatula or an electric hand mixer on a medium speed for 5–10 minutes until soft and creamy. Gradually mix in the eggs, beating well between each addition.

3. Add the flour, baking powder and salt and, using the spatula, fold the dry ingredients into the creamed mixture until well combined. Mix in the milk, 10g (¼ oz) at a time, until the mixture has a dropping consistency.

4. Transfer the mixture to the prepared tin and smooth the top using a palette knife. Arrange the fig slices on the top of the cake in an even layer and sprinkle the Demerara sugar over the top.

5. Bake for 30–40 minutes or until a skewer inserted into the centre comes out clean. Cool in the tin before serving. The cake can be stored in the fridge for up to three days but bring it to room temperature before serving.

BLOOD ORANGE POLENTA CAKE

February is the month I most wish I were back in Australia. Since I am in the UK, and not there, I find pleasure in the blood oranges and pink rhubarb and the slowly lengthening days when the grey of February seems interminable. The seasons really confront you in the UK – I had once been used to them failing to announce their arrival or departure except by the calendar. Blood orange polenta cake is one of our counter staples; a similar cake features in independent cafés the world over. It's beloved by customers and as a cake with neither dairy or wheat, is much in demand, and this a particularly good example of the genre. Use any other oranges when blood oranges are not available and try lemons too.

MAKES 1 CAKE

54g (2 oz) extra virgin olive oil
161g (5½ oz) sunflower oil
287g (10¼ oz) caster sugar
2 large blood oranges,
finely zested
258g (9 oz)/5 whole eggs,
beaten
143g (5 oz) polenta
10g (¼ oz) gluten free baking
powder
287g (10¼ oz) ground almonds

For the syrup
juice of 2 large blood oranges
approximately 100g caster
sugar (to match weight of
orange juice)

1. Preheat the oven to 160ºC/325ºF/ gas mark 3. Line a loaf tin with baking parchment.

2. Place the oils, sugar and zest in a medium bowl or a freestanding mixer with paddle attachment. Mix with a handheld electric mixer or on low to medium speed for 3–4 minutes. Don't overmix as if there is too much aeration at this stage the cake may collapse in the oven. Gradually add the egg while the whisk or mixer is running, in 3 or 4 additions; the mixture should emulsify and appear smooth and glossy.

3. Add the polenta, baking powder and ground almonds and mix at low speed until incorporated. Transfer the mixture to the prepared tin.

4. Bake for 60–70 minutes. Don't open the oven for the first 50 minutes of baking time to avoid the cake collapsing.

5. While the cake is baking, prepare the orange syrup. Weigh the juice from the oranges and place in a small saucepan with an equal weight of caster sugar. Heat over a low heat until the sugar dissolves and then bring to the boil and remove from the heat. Allow to cool.

6. When the cake comes out of the oven, allow it to cool for 30 minutes in the tin and then pour the syrup over the cake. When the cake is completely cool, remove from the tin.

MARINA'S APRICOT LAVENDER SLICE

When I made cakes for a living, the business was called The Lavender Bakery because I love lavender in sweet baked goods. I often make the apricot and lavender jam from my beloved copy of Diana Henry's book, *Salt Sugar Smoke*, and this recipe started with the desire to use a favourite flavour combination with the easy, fruity slices of my Australian childhood. Marina is the pastry chef at Margot and when we started to develop the recipe it took a Polish twist based on her mother's recipe for *Jabłecznik*. It is a simple, soft pastry with a filling of not-too-sweet fruit. I have had Polish staff and customers at Margot since the very beginning (Joanna, Marta, Samuel, Milena, Anna; hello!) and have thus been introduced to the wonders of Polish food and their insatiable love of baked goods; and I can now fluently swear in Polish too.

MAKES 12 SLICES
20cm (8 in)

For the filling
2kg (4½ lb) fresh apricots
3 tsp dried edible lavender flowers
200g (7 oz) caster sugar

For the dough
440g (15½ oz) plain flour
180g (6¼ oz) caster sugar
10g (¼ oz) baking powder
360g (12½ oz) unsalted butter, chilled and cut into 2cm (¾ in) cubes
66g (2½ oz) full fat Greek yoghurt
80g (3 oz)/4 egg yolks
60g (2½ oz) Demerara sugar
60g (2½ oz) flaked almonds (optional)

1. Prepare the filling in advance, so it has at least an hour to cool before assembling the slice. Stone and roughly chop the apricots and place in a medium pan with the lavender and sugar over a low to medium heat with a lid on. Cook for 10–15 minutes until the sugar has dissolved, remove the lid, turn up the heat a little and cook for another 5–10 minutes. The apricots should be softened but still holding some shape. Set aside to cool.

2. Preheat the oven to 200ºC/400ºF/gas mark 6. Line a 20 cm (8 in) square cake tin with baking parchment.

3. For the dough place the flour, caster sugar, baking powder and butter in a medium bowl or a freestanding mixer with paddle attachment. Rub between your fingertips or mix on low speed until the mixture resembles fine breadcrumbs

4. Add the yoghurt and egg yolks and mix by hand or on low speed until a smooth, sticky dough forms. Divide the dough in half, wrap one half in clingfilm and place in the fridge.

5. Take small pieces of the remaining dough, flatten in your hands into small discs and arrange so they overlap slightly in the bottom of the lined tin. Press down to form an even layer and prick all over with a fork. Bake for 20 minutes until golden brown. Allow to cool.

6. Spread the apricot filling over the baked dough in an even layer. Take the remaining dough from the fridge and form small discs as before, laying over the fruit in an even layer. No need to push down – there should be gaps between the discs.

7. Sprinkle with Demerara sugar and flaked almonds, if using. Bake for an additional 20–25 minutes until the top is golden brown. Cool in the tin and then cut into 12 slices.

PERLETTE'S APPLE CAKE

Perlette was my husband, Victor's grandmother; a formidable and passionate woman who lived an extraordinary life, including time spent with the French Resistance during WW2. She spoke French and little English and I speak English and little French so the only topic that we were easily able to communicate on was baking. I understood just enough baking-related French words to follow her descriptions and I now cherish those few recipes she described to me. Before she stopped baking in her later years I tasted this cake made by her, known by Victor as Nanny's Gateau Aux Pommes. I had to take my memory of eating it and the few words of French description offered to come up with a recipe; it's defining feature being an extraordinary quantity of apple in proportion to cake. I hope my boys, who often speak of their Grande Nanny, can keep their connection with her a little closer through eating, and one day baking, this cake.

MAKES 1 CAKE
25cm (10 in)

For the apples
2.7kg (6 lb) crisp eating apples, such as Cox's or Braeburn
190g (6¾ oz) caster sugar
20g (¾ oz) ground cinnamon
squeeze of lemon juice

For the cake
180g (6¼ oz) unsalted butter
225g (8 oz) vanilla caster sugar
270g (9½ oz)/5½ whole eggs, beaten
255g (9 oz) plain flour
4g (⅛ oz) sea salt
10g (¼ oz) ground cinnamon
100g (3½ oz) caster sugar

1. Preheat the oven to 160°C/325°F/gas mark 3. Line a 25cm (10 in) round cake tin with baking parchment.

2. Core, peel and roughly chop two thirds of the apples. Cook in a medium pan, with the sugar and cinnamon, until soft but holding their shape, roughly 15–20 minutes. Set aside to cool.

3. Core and thinly slice the remaining apples and place in a bowl of cold water with a squeeze of lemon juice.

4. Place the butter in a small pan and gently melt over a very low heat. Strain through a fine sieve to remove the solids, which can be discarded. Set the strained butter aside to cool.

5. Place the vanilla sugar and eggs in a medium bowl or a free standing mixer. With a handheld electric mixer or with the mixer whisk attachment, whisk until pale and thick and the mixture holds thin ribbons on the surface when the whisk is lifted.

6. Sift the flour and salt together and add half to the mixture. Fold in gently with a spatula until no flour is visible. Repeat with the remaining flour and salt and then fold in 150g (5 oz) cooled, melted butter.

7. Spoon just over half the cake mixture into the prepared tin and spoon over the cooled, cooked apple in an even layer. Arrange half the raw apple slices, in a single layer, on top of the cooked apple and top with the remaining cake mixture. Arrange the remaining apple slices in a circular pattern on top and sprinkle over the cinnamon and caster sugar.

8. Bake for 70–90 minutes or until a skewer inserted into the centre comes out clean. Cool in the tin. The cake is delicious both warm or cool. It should be stored in the fridge if it isn't eaten with 24 hours.

CHOCOLATE CAKE WITH CHOCOLATE GLAZE

My children have high expectations of what I am able to achieve in cake terms when their birthdays come around (it was not great planning that they were born two years and two days apart), but I can usually get away with a simply decorated, delicious cake if I quickly redirect them when their ideas start to sound very time consuming. For my eldest's sixth birthday he requested a hexagon-shaped chocolate cake with chocolate icing and an Eiffel Tower; this was the chocolate cake I made and it's the only chocolate cake I ever bake. It pleases adults and children alike being chocolatey but not heavy, and it holds its shape well so can be made into a loaf cake, a layer cake or even cupcakes. It is a regular on the counter and we bake them to order for customers, covered with vanilla Italian meringue buttercream frosting or this glaze.

MAKES 1 CAKE
20cm (8 in)

For the cake
300g (11 oz) plain flour
½ tsp baking powder
6g (¼ oz) sea salt
6g (¼ oz) bicarbonate of soda
113g (4 oz) cocoa powder
180g (6¼ oz) hot coffee
180g (6¼ oz) cold water
170g (6 oz) unsalted butter, at room temperature
411g (14½ oz) caster sugar
134g (4½ oz)/2½ whole eggs, lightly beaten

For the chocolate glaze
270g (9½ oz) dark chocolate, roughly chopped
183g (6½ oz) unsalted butter, roughly chopped
30g (1 oz) glucose or golden syrup

1. Preheat the oven to 160ºC/325ºF/gas mark 3. Grease and line 2 x 20cm (8 in) round cake tins with baking parchment.

2. Sift the flour, baking powder, salt and bicarbonate of soda into a medium bowl.

3. Whisk the hot coffee into the cocoa powder until a smooth paste is formed. Add the cold water and whisk again until well combined and lump free.

4. Place the butter and sugar in a medium bowl or a free standing mixer with paddle attachment. Beat with a spatula, an electric hand mixer or on medium speed for 5–10 minutes until soft and creamy. Gradually mix in the eggs, beating well between each addition.

5. Add one third of the flour mixture to the butter mix and stir to combine. Then add one third of the cocoa mixture, mix well and scrape down the edge of the bowl. Repeat the process until all the ingredients are fully incorporated. Divide the mixture equally between the cake tins.

6. Bake for 40 minutes until a skewer inserted in the centre comes out clean. The cakes should be gently domed and coming away from the sides of the tin.

7. While the cakes are baking, prepare the glaze by placing all the ingredients in a small heatproof bowl over a pan of barely simmering water. Stir occasionally until the butter is melted and the mix is smooth and glossy. Transfer half the mixture to a small bowl and place it in the fridge. Set the remaining bowl of glaze aside at room temperature.

8. Allow the cakes to cool for 30 minutes in the tins and then turn then out onto a wire cooling rack and carefully peel off the baking parchment while still warm.

9. When the cakes are almost completely cool lay one of the sponges on a serving plate, top side down. Using a knife or the back on a spoon spread the chilled glaze over the cake, taking it in gentle waves almost to the outer edge. Turn the second cake upside down as with the first, and place on top of the glazed sponge.

10. Refrigerate the cake for 30–40 minutes, or longer if it suits you, before applying the final poured glaze.

11. If the remaining glaze has set too much so that it cannot be poured, warm it gently over a pan of warm water until runny but not too liquid. Pour the glaze all over the top of the cake. It will set into a shiny glaze when chilled or will stay soft if kept out of the fridge.

12. Store the cake in the fridge but bring to room temperature before serving.

CHOCOLATE CAKE WITH CHOCOLATE GLAZE

MARGOT SPECIALITIES

BLUEBERRY BUNDT WITH FONDANT ICING

I should have done my degree in Psychology because so much of my time at the bakery is spent evaluating what customers would like to buy, on which days and in what quantities. Customers hardly notice the full display; they look at a few key places on the counter and shelves and so adding colour and height to the counter and display makes cakes sell better than they otherwise might. The beautiful distinctive ring shape of a bundt cake with its tender crumb exposed is always a winner, with the addition of edible flowers the customers can't resist.

Take the time to prepare the tin as described and your bundt cake will slide out perfectly. Should there be a disaster, you will understand what icing is useful in a bakery.

MAKES 1 CAKE
25cm (10 in)

For the sponge
40g (1½ oz) butter, for greasing
flour, for dusting
30g (1 oz) full fat Greek yoghurt
240g (8½ oz)/5 whole eggs, beaten
280g (10 oz) plain white flour
8g (¼ oz) baking powder
225g (8 oz) unsalted butter, at room temperature
½ vanilla pod, split and scraped
zest of ½ lemon or ½ orange
225g (8 oz) cream cheese
330g (11½ oz) caster sugar
180g (6¼ oz) fresh blueberries, washed and dried

For the icing
400g (14 oz) icing sugar
20g (¾ oz) glucose
juice of 1 lemon or 1 orange
(blood oranges give a lovely colour, when in season)
fresh berries, to decorate
edible leaves and flowers, to decorate

1. First, prepare the tin. Melt the butter for greasing the bundt tin in a small saucepan. With a pastry brush apply the butter to all parts of the tin. Place in the freezer for 15 minutes. Remove from the freezer, paint another layer of butter onto the tin and put a small handful of flour into the tin and rotate the tin so the flour sticks to the butter layer. Tap out any excess flour and set aside. Alternatively, you can use a 25cm (10 in) round cake tin, greased and lined with baking parchment.

2. Preheat the oven to 160°C/325°F/gas mark 3. Place the yoghurt and eggs in a small bowl. Sift the flour and baking powder into another bowl.

3. Place the butter, vanilla seeds and zest in a medium bowl or free standing mixer with paddle attachment. Beat with an electric hand mixer or on medium speed for 7–8 minutes, until very soft and pale. Add the cream cheese and mix until combined. Add the sugar and mix 5 minutes until the mix is pale and light.

4. Add the beaten eggs and yoghurt and mix briefly, on a low speed, then firmly and gently, fold in the sifted ingredients by hand, until the mix is well combined.

5. Drop spoonfuls of batter into the cake tin and scatter the blueberries on top – they will sink into the cake during baking.

6. Bake for 50–55 minutes or until a skewer inserted into the deepest part of the cake comes out clean.

7. Turn the cake out onto a wire cooling rack while it is still slightly warm, before the butter has completely cooled. Allow to cool completely before icing.

8. To make the icing, place the sugar and glucose in a medium heatproof bowl and add a few drops of juice at a time, stirring until it no longer looks dry. It should be slightly thicker than pouring consistency as it will liquefy with warming. It's better to add less, rather than more, liquid.

9. Place the bowl of icing over a pan of gently simmering water stirring regularly. Use a sugar thermometer to check when mixture has reached 37–38°C (98–100°F). When it is neither hot nor cold to the touch remove from heat. It will have a shinier finish if it does not get too warm.

10. Pour a little icing over an upturned bowl, it should run down the sides but stops before it quite reaches the bottom. If it is too runny add a little more icing sugar and warm slightly. If it is too thick add a little more juice. When you are satisfied pour the icing over the cake. While the icing is slightly soft, arrange the berries, leaves and flowers on top. Serve.

MIXED FRUIT AND POPPY SEED STRUDEL

Strudel dough is so satisfying to handle – it needs to be stretched until it is extraordinarily thin and covers a table. A short film, shared by my customer Kata, of her grandma deftly handling the dough on her kitchen table and rolling strudel with a dedicated strudel cloth spurred me to make my own and I have gathered tips and details from Hungarian staff too; thank you Diana and Gyorgyi! Hungarian strudel can be filled with sweet fillings such as apple, poppy seeds or sour cherries, or with savoury fillings such as egg, cabbage or cheese. This is a version we have made at Margot with fruit filling and poppy seeds; I make no claims to its authenticity but it is a good starting point for experimentation. The filling should be made a day in advance.

MAKES 1 STRUDEL

For the filling
150g (5 oz) poppy seeds
800g (1¾ lb) eating apples, cored and roughly chopped, with skin on
squeeze of lemon juice
15g (½ oz) caster sugar
225g (8 oz) Demerara sugar
200g (7 oz) raisins
100g (3½ oz) currants

For the dough
166g (5¾ oz) white bread flour, plus extra for dusting
50g (2 oz)/1 whole egg
78g (3 oz) cold water
a large pinch of sea salt
1 tsp sunflower oil, plus extra for greasing
100g (3½ oz) unsalted butter

1. The day before you are planning to bake the strudel, make the filling. Place the poppy seeds in a pan of water, bring to the boil and then simmer for 1 hour. Place the apples, lemon juice and caster sugar in a medium pan, cover and cook gently for 20 minutes then transfer to a medium bowl. Drain the poppy seeds and grind in a food processor or blender and add to a bowl along with the apples and the Demerara sugar, raisins and currants. Stir well, cover and set aside overnight.

2. Place the flour, egg, water, salt and oil in a medium bowl or in a free standing mixer fitted with a dough hook. Mix until a rough dough forms and then switch to a medium speed for 8–10 minutes. Alternatively, knead the dough by hand on an unfloured work surface until the dough is smooth and strong. Place in a lightly oiled bowl, cover and allow to rest for 30–60 minutes at room temperature.

3. When you are ready to start assembling the strudel, preheat the oven to 190ºC/375ºF/gas mark 5. Line a large baking tray with baking parchment.

4. Place the butter in a small pan and heat gently until melted. Spread a clean tablecloth out on a table and dust it lightly with flour.

5. Place the dough in the centre of the tablecloth, dip your fingers in the melted butter and splash a little onto the dough. Start to stretch the dough from the centre, outwards – you are aiming for a piece of dough approximately 50 x 60cm (20 x 23½ in). Make your way around the table and stretch the dough evenly on all sides. Use your hands facing down so the dough stretches over your knuckles, which are less likely to make holes than your fingertips. If the dough starts to tear or feels like it won't easily stretch, then wait 5–10 minutes and go back to stretching.

6. When you have a thin, even layer of dough about 50 x 60cm (20 x 23½in), tear or trim the thicker edge off the dough and brush the dough all over with melted butter.

7. Scatter the filling evenly all over the dough, and using the tablecloth, lift one of the 60cm (23½ in) edges and begin to gently roll the strudel up. Tuck the edges under, at either end, to close them. When you have a long roll, pick it up and either curve it into a horseshoe shape and place on the lined tray or cut it in half and lay the two pieces side by side on the tray.

8. Brush again with melted butter and bake for 30–35 minutes until golden brown. The strudel is best served warm.

MARGOT SPECIALITIES

CUSTARD TART WITH CARAMELISED BREADCRUMBS

When I was a child, the cookbook in our house that I most loved was the Australian Women's Weekly *Big Book of Beautiful Biscuits*. I have the copy in my possession now though it is falling apart a little, some pages have my Mum's notes scribbled on them and flicking through it gives me waves of nostalgia. I credit a desire to make the meringue mice and snails in this book with my eventual career in baking. We had baking essentials at home; orange scales and an orange electric hand mixer, remnants of the seventies fashion in homewares, the decade when my parents received them as wedding gifts. My Mum baked occasionally and well, her specialties being Pavlova and egg custard; I remember its wobble and the grating of nutmeg on top. This recipe is the Margot version of a childhood favourite. Be warned though, the caramelised breadcrumbs are addictive.

MAKES 1 TART
25cm (10 in)

For the breadcrumbs
350g (12 oz) stale sourdough bread (approximately half a loaf), crusts removed
50g (2 oz) Demerara sugar
50g (2 oz) unsalted butter

For the pastry
470g (1 lb ½ oz) plain flour, plus extra for dusting
large pinch of salt
95g (3¼ oz) vanilla caster sugar
235g (8¼ oz) unsalted butter, chilled and cut into 1cm (½ in) cubes
65g (2½ oz)/3 egg yolks
75g (3 oz) ice cold water

For the custard filling
240g (8½ oz) whole milk
500g (1 lb 2 oz) double cream
½ vanilla pod, split and scraped
95g (3¼ oz) vanilla caster sugar
100g (3½ oz)/5 medium egg yolks
70g (2¾ oz)/1½ medium whole eggs

1. Preheat the oven to 200ºC/400ºF/gas mark 6.

2. To make the breadcrumbs, tear the bread into small pieces and place in a bowl with the sugar. Melt the butter in a small pan and pour over the bread and sugar. Stir well to coat. Scatter on a baking tray lined with parchment and bake for 15–20 minutes. Remove from the oven when the pieces of bread are golden on the edges and crunchy. When cool, pulse in a food processor or chop with a sharp knife. Don't make the breadcrumbs too small, you want some texture.

3. To make the pastry, place the flour, salt, sugar and butter in a medium bowl or in a free standing mixer with paddle attachment. Rub between your fingertips or mix on low speed until the mix resembles fine breadcrumbs. Add the egg yolks and water and bring together with your hand until a dough forms. Knead the dough with the heel of your hand on the work surface until smooth. Form into a disc, wrap and refrigerate for 1 hour.

4. On a lightly floured surface, roll the pastry outwards from the centre, turning it by a quarter with each roll, to make a circle slightly bigger than a 25cm (10 in) tin or ring. If using a pastry ring, place it on a baking tray lined with parchment. Line the tin or ring with the pastry, pushing gently into the corners. Chill for 30–60 minutes.

5. Preheat the oven to 180ºC/350ºF/gas mark 4.

6. Trim the top edges of pastry, with a sharp knife, and prick the base all over with a fork. Place a circle of baking parchment on top of the pastry and fill to the top with baking beans or dried beans. Bake for 15 minutes then remove the paper and beans and bake for a further 5–10 minutes, until the pastry is golden and crisp. Set the pastry case aside to cool. Reduce the oven temperature to 150ºC/300ºF/gas mark 2.

7. Place the milk, cream, vanilla seeds and pod in a small pan. Bring to a boil, remove the vanilla pod. Put the sugar, yolks and whole egg in a medium heatproof bowl then pour the milk and cream mix over, whisking constantly. Strain through a fine strainer into a jug.

8. Scatter the caramelised breadcrumbs over the pastry base. Carefully pour the custard into the tart case and transfer to the oven. Bake for 25–35 minutes until set but still wobbly in the middle. Cool then chill and serve cold.

CHEESE AND ONION PIE

Since opening, customers often ask for Margot or call me Margot. I didn't know that this would happen but I answer to Margot too now. When I named the bakery I was looking for something that communicated warmth, community and a different approach to baking. Various ideas were discarded in conversation with Lucy, designer and architect for the bakery, but Margot resonated as it made me think of two wonderful women, my husband's grandmother Perlette, or Perla, and my Nana, Margaret. The Greek and Latin words for Pearl are the root of the names Margot, Margaret, and Pearl. My Nana, though not a baker, is from Oldham in Lancashire, and has been a constant kind and generous presence in my life along with my grandfather. This pie connects me to the place I was born and I think of my northern family when I make it.

MAKES 1 PIE
25cm (10 in)

For the filling
1.2kg (2 lb 10¼ oz) brown onions, peeled and finely sliced in half moon shapes.
60g (2½ oz) unsalted butter
1 medium bunch of fresh thyme
800g (1¾ lb) Lancashire cheese, thickly sliced
salt and freshly ground black pepper

For the hot water crust pastry
175g (6 oz) unsalted butter
170g (6 oz) water
463g (1lb ¼ oz) strong white bread flour, plus extra for dusting
125g (4 oz)/2½ whole eggs
1 tsp sea salt
beaten egg, to glaze

1. To make the filling, place the sliced onions, butter and 1 tsp salt in a medium saucepan. Cover and cook gently for 30–40 minutes, over a low heat, until soft and wilted. Set aside a few whole thyme sprigs (for garnishing the pie) and strip the leaves from the remaining sprigs. Remove the lid from the onions, add half the thyme leaves and season lightly; cook for another 15–20 minutes until the onions have dried out a little. Cool and check the seasoning. The onions should be meltingly soft and quite sweet but well seasoned.

2. For the pastry, place the butter and water in a small saucepan over a low to medium heat until the butter is just melted. Allow to cool for 20 minutes before using.

3. Place the flour, eggs and salt in a medium bowl or in free standing mixer fitted with a dough hook. Begin to mix and when the eggs and flour are well combined, pour in the water and butter mix, stirring constantly, for 3–4 minutes until the dough is smooth or knead on a work surface for 4–5 minutes. Transfer to a bowl and cover. Rest for at least 30 minutes or up to 2 hours.

4. Preheat the oven to 180ºC/350ºF/gas mark 4.

5. Divide the pastry into two pieces, one twice the size of the other.

6. On a lightly floured surface, roll the larger piece of pastry into a circle slightly larger than a 25cm (10 in) pie dish. Transfer to the dish by rolling the dough over the rolling pin and unrolling it carefully over the pie dish. Push into the corners but leave the edges overhanging the dish.

7. Arrange a layer of cooled onion at the bottom of the dish then a layer of cheese. Add black pepper and a sprinkle of thyme leaves as you build the layers. Continue with the layers of cheese and onion until all the ingredients are used up.

8. Roll out your remaining piece of dough into a circle a little larger than the top diameter of your pie dish and place on top of the pie. Trim the edges and pinch them together – you can make a pattern or just firmly press to close them.

9. Brush with the beaten egg and arrange the reserved thyme sprigs on top of the pie, making sure they make good contact with the pastry.

10. Make several holes in the top with a knife so steam can escape and bake for 50–70 minutes until hot, golden and the cheese is bubbling. Serve warm or cold.

MARGOT SPECIALITIES

GOAT'S CHEESE, PEAR AND WALNUT GALETTE

My accountant, Jane, steers me through the complexities of VAT and my many other queries with good humour and vast knowledge, and I am not sure I could have got through the first years of business without her help. Did you know that if an item is hot because it is freshly baked and then allowed to cool naturally, one can sell it for takeaway consumption without adding VAT? If one were to keep it hot, reheat it or if the customer sits down at a table to enjoy it then VAT must be added. Many of our products have been developed so that they can be baked in the morning and almost immediately transferred to the counter for sale mid morning through to lunchtime. The beauty of this galette dough is that it is equally as delicious cold as hot.

MAKES 1 GALETTE
30cm (12 in)

For the dough
488g (1lb 1¼ oz) strong
white bread flour, plus extra
for dusting
355g (12½ oz) unsalted butter,
chilled and cut into 2cm (¾ in)
cubes
7g (¼ oz) sea salt
110g (3¾ oz) water
190g (6¾ oz) full fat
Greek yoghurt
25g (1 oz) white wine vinegar

For the filling
600g (1 lb 5 oz) firm mild
goat's cheese
8–10 firm, ripe pears
(depending on size) cored and
sliced, with skin on
1 small bunch of fresh thyme
30ml (1 ½ fl oz) olive oil
salt and freshly ground black
pepper
beaten egg, to glaze

1. To make the dough, place the flour, butter and salt in a medium bowl or in a freestanding mixer with the paddle attachment fitted. Rub between your fingertips or mix on low speed until the mixture resembles fine breadcrumbs.

2. Mix the water and yoghurt in a small bowl and add to the flour mix. Add the vinegar and mix with a spoon or on low speed until the dough comes together. Knead for 5–8 minutes on a work surface or on medium speed.

3. Shape the dough into a fat disc and wrap in clingfilm and then refrigerate for at least 1 hour or up to 2 days.

4. Preheat the oven to 200ºC/400ºF/gas mark 6. Line a baking tray with baking parchment.

5. Remove the dough from the fridge and roll on a lightly floured work surface into a large rectangle approximately 25 x 40cm (10 x 16 in). Take care the dough does not stick to the counter as you roll; use as much flour as needed underneath.

6. Transfer the dough to the lined tray. Leaving a 2.5cm (1 in) border around the edges, arrange pieces of goat's cheese, slices of pear and thyme leaves over the dough. Drizzle with the oil and season well with salt and pepper. Fold the edges over onto the filling to create a border around the sides, leaving the centre visible. Brush the folded edges with the beaten egg.

7. Bake for 30–35 minutes until the cheese is bubbling and the edges of the dough are a rich golden brown. Serve hot, warm or cold.

LAMINGTONS

Lamingtons are arguably the most recognisable Australian cake and are named after Lord Lamington, a British governor of Queensland in the nineteenth and early twentieth century. Many traditional recipes were developed in a time when ingredients were expensive relative to income, and chocolate coloured icing rather than what could reasonably be described as actual chocolate icing is often used for lamingtons. If you use excellent quality butter, eggs and chocolate and if you like coconut, they are fantastic. Embrace the mess – there's no tidy way to go about making them. I make them now for Anzac day at the bakery; making them for 26 January, which is designated as Australia day, and also Invasion day by Indigenous Australians, is problematic and seems insensitive. I hope soon a new date satisfactory to all can be agreed upon.

MAKES 20 LAMINGTONS

For the sponge
423g (15 oz) plain flour
14g (½ oz) baking powder
4g (⅛ oz) salt
216g (7½ oz) unsalted butter, at room temperature
434g (15¼ oz) caster sugar
1 tsp vanilla extract
115g (4 oz)/7 egg yolks
343g (12 oz) whole milk

For the icing
40g (1½ oz) cocoa powder
285g (10 oz) whole milk
10g (¼ oz) glucose
460g (1lb ¼ oz) dark chocolate, broken into rough chunks
27g (1 oz) unsalted butter
275g (10 oz) icing sugar

To assemble
400g (14 oz) desiccated coconut

1. Preheat the oven to 160°C/325°F/gas mark 3. Grease and line a 25cm (10 in) square tin with baking parchment.

2. Sift the flour, baking powder and salt into a bowl and set aside.

3. Cream the butter, sugar and vanilla together in a mixer with paddle attachment or in a bowl with a handheld electric mixer for 10 minutes, until very pale and fluffy. Add the egg yolks in 2 or 3 additions until well mixed. Add half the flour mix and mix on a very low speed or fold in with a spatula. Add half the milk and fold through. Repeat with the remaining flour and milk.

4. Place the mixture in the prepared tin and level the top with the back of a spoon. Bake for 35–40 minutes until the top springs back when pressed lightly and a skewer inserted into the centre comes out clean.

5. Turn the sponge out onto a wire cooling rack and allow to cool completely. Assemble the lamingtons on the same day or wrap the sponge in clingfilm, store at room temperature and use within 2 days.

6. To make the icing, dissolve the cocoa powder in 3–4 tbsp of the milk, blending to form a smooth paste. Place the paste in a large heatproof bowl with the glucose and chocolate.

7. Place the remaining milk in a medium pan with the butter and icing sugar and heat until almost boiling. Pour the milk mixture over the cocoa paste and stir with a whisk until smooth. Allow to cool a little – it will thicken as it cools. If you need to make it runnier again, place the bowl over a pan of gently simmering water.

8. To assemble the lamingtons, trim the sponge on all sides and divide it into 20 equal rectangles. Use a ruler to mark where you will cut. After trimming, divide the length of one side by 4 and the other side by 5.

9. Transfer one third of the icing to a small bowl. Place one third of the coconut in another small bowl. Use a fork to help you dip rectangles of sponge first in chocolate sauce and then roll the rectangle in coconut. Place on a wire cooling rack to set. Top up the bowls with fresh icing and coconut, as needed.

10. Once set, transfer to an airtight container and store at room temperature for up to 3 days.

JAMS AND SPREADS

CRÈME PÂTISSIÈRE

With thanks to my friend, the pastry chef Ravneet Gill for this recipe. It can be used alone, baked or chilled, combined with cream cheese at a ratio of 20% cream cheese to crème pâtissière, or after chilling folded with 50% whipped double cream to make a delicious pastry or doughnut filling. We also use it for poppy seed Babka (see page 112) and to make Pain aux raisins (see page 88). Crème pâtissière is a useful part of a baker's repertoire.

MAKES 400G (14 OZ)

30g (1 oz)/½ whole egg
30g (1 oz)/2 egg yolks
70g (2¾ oz) caster sugar
20g (¾ oz) cornflour
80g (3 oz) double cream
185g (6½ oz) whole milk
¼ vanilla pod, split and scraped, or ½ tsp vanilla extract

1. Put the whole egg and egg yolks into a medium heatproof bowl with the sugar. Mix briefly and then add the cornflour and mix briefly again.

2. Place 1 tsp water in the bottom of a medium saucepan (this stops the milk burning) and add the cream, milk and vanilla. Bring to the boil.

3. Pour half the milk mixture over the egg mixture, whisking constantly as you pour. And the remaining milk mixture and then return the crème pâtissière to the pan and whisk over a medium heat until it thickens.

4. Push the crème pâtissière through a fine sieve, if you want it very smooth.

5. Transfer the crème pâtissière to a glass or plastic container, cover with a piece of clingfilm pressed onto the surface (to prevent a skin forming) and cool. Chill in the fridge for up to 3 days.

ALMOND FRANGIPANE

One of our bakers, Alvaro, did a test last year to establish whether salt made any difference to frangipane and his verdict was that it does. He made two batches side by side, one with salt and one without. A pinch of salt in most cakes enhances the flavour and this is also true of frangipane. It can be used in Almond Croissants (see page 102) of course but also to fill tarts.

MAKES 300G (11 OZ)

75g (3 oz) unsalted butter, at room temperature
75g (3 oz) caster sugar
75g (3 oz) ground almonds
pinch of salt
75g (3 oz)/1½ whole eggs, beaten

1. Place the butter, sugar, ground nuts and salt in a bowl. With a handheld electric mixer or a spatula combine until soft and slightly creamy. Gradually add the beaten eggs and mix until combined. Chill if not using immediately

DIFFERENT FLAVOURS OF FRANGIPANE

Follow the basic frangipane recipe, but use the following instead of the almonds:

- **Hazelnut and chocolate:** 65g (2½ oz) toasted ground hazelnuts and 10g (¼ oz) dark cocoa powder.
- **Pistachio:** 75g (3 oz) toasted ground unsalted pistachios.
- **Tahini** 75g (3 oz) tahini.

JAMS AND SPREADS

LEMON CURD

Occasionally we use zest from oranges and lemons at the bakery for bread or cakes and end up with a glut of zested, but otherwise usable citrus fruits, which is where lemon curd comes in handy. Use any citrus fruit or a blend; bergamot, when in season, are delightful, or try oranges or even clementines.

MAKES 400G (14 OZ)

95g (3½ oz)/2 whole eggs
30g (1 oz)/2 egg yolks
130g (4½ oz) caster sugar
65g (2½ oz) unsalted butter,
chilled and roughly cubed
juice from 3–4 lemons
(approximately 96g (3½ oz)
zest from 2 lemons
(approximately 4g (⅛ oz)

1. In a medium pan over a low heat, whisk the whole eggs, egg yolks and sugar until the sugar dissolves.

2. Add the butter, lemon zest and juice to the pan, stirring frequently – especially as the mix heats up and approaches boiling point. Remove from the heat just before it comes to the boil, when thickened.

3. If using for baking, transfer to a container, cool and refrigerate for up to 5 days.

4. Alternatively, to store for longer, sterilise a jar by washing it in hot soapy water and rinsing it well. Place on a baking tray and put in the oven. Turn the oven to 110°C/225°F/gas mark ¼. When the oven has heated up, leave it on for 15 minutes, then turn it off, leaving the jar inside until cool. Transfer the curd to the sterilised jar, and store in the fridge.

SIMPLE SYRUP

MAKES 300G (11 OZ)

200g (7 oz) granulated sugar
100g (1½ oz) water

Place the sugar and water in a small saucepan, over a low heat, stir occasionally. When the liquid is clear and the sugar has dissolved, bring to the boil and then remove from the heat. Set aside to cool and then add the flavouring, if using. Store in the fridge until needed.

FLAVOURING THE SUGAR SYRUP

Add any of the following to the syrup:

- 50g (2 oz) espresso coffee
- 150g (5 oz) freshly squeezed lemon juice
- 150g (5 oz) freshly squeezed orange juice
- 100g (3½ oz) raspberry purée
- 1 vanilla pod, split and scaped, or a few drops of vanilla extract

FERMENTED RED PEPPER, TOMATO AND CHILLI

A jar of fermented pepper, tomato and chilli has become a staple in my fridge. It is useful in many dishes and this version was inspired by the ingredients in the Middle Eastern dip Muhammara. It is magical to watch the transformation of simple ingredients through the invisible toil of yeast and bacteria. I often use kefir for fermentation and baking and lacto-fermentation is also a great way to not only preserve fruit and vegetables but to create more complex flavours; there are health benefits, too, in adding fermented foods to the diet.

This works well with some bread, eggs and a yoghurt dip for lunch, or as a condiment alongside other dishes.

MAKES 1 LITRE (1¾ PINTS)

20g (¾ oz) sea salt
1 litre (1¾ pints) water
250g (9 oz) ripe baby plum tomatoes, washed
500g (1 lb 2 oz) red peppers, deseeded and sliced
3 garlic cloves, peeled
100g (3½ oz) hot red chillies, deseeded and sliced into 1cm (¼ in) rounds

For the dip (optional)
150g (5 oz) finely chopped toasted walnuts
50g (2 oz) extra virgin olive oil
small bunch of parsley, finely chopped

1. Place the salt and water in a pan over a medium heat, and stir until the salt dissolves. Bring to the boil and cool.

2. Pierce the tomatoes in the side using a small, sharp knife. Place the prepared vegetables, in layers, in a cool, sterilised jar (see page 205), pushing them down as far as you can. Pour the cooled salt water over the vegetables until it fills the jar. Place a circle of baking parchment at the top of the jar and place something small and heavy, like a small bowl, on top of the paper to push the vegetables under the level of the water. This ensures the vegetables can ferment safely, deprived of oxygen.

3. Set aside in a warm place for 2–3 days or up to a week. Taste and if you would like it to ferment further give it more time. In summer the process will be quicker and in winter, slower. When you are happy with the flavour – it will get increasingly tangy – transfer to the fridge where it will keep for several weeks.

4. You can serve the vegetables whole or pulse in a food processor to make a coarsely textured sauce to be used as a condiment.

5. To make the dip (optional), roughly chop 300g (11 oz) red pepper, tomato and chilli and combine in a bowl with the chopped walnuts, olive oil and parsley. Taste for seasoning – if it is not spicy enough add some chilli flakes. If it is too tangy add some date syrup to balance the flavours.

BEETROOT AND CARAWAY JAM

My youngest son adores beetroot, feta, avocado and tahini, none of which my eldest will touch. Both children love pickles, raw vegetables and smoked salmon and my eldest dislikes cheese but loves kale salad more than seems right for an eight year old. They both eat to their appetites and to their preferences, which pleases me; they like to bake and to cook and are learning to season food properly; if I give them nothing else then I will have given them confidence in engaging with the pleasure, language, memories and conversations that happen around food in a home and in a business. If I make this for my youngest then I don't make it spicy and will omit the caraway; if I make it for me, or at the bakery, then I do.

Use the jam to make Smoked Cheese and Beetroot Pull Apart Bread (page 154) or dollop on a sandwich with smoked salmon or a sharp Cheddar.

MAKES 2 X 300G (11 OZ) JARS

1kg (2¼ lb) beetroot, peeled and cut into 3–4cm (1¼–1½ in) pieces
30ml (1fl oz) olive oil
1 large red onion, thinly sliced
1 tsp caraway seeds
2–3 pinches dried chilli flakes
200g (7 oz) dark brown sugar
100g (3½ oz) red wine vinegar
salt
dill, to serve

1. Preheat the oven to 180°C/350°F/gas mark 4. Line a baking tray with baking parchment.

2. Place the beetroot on the lined tray, drizzle half of the oil over and season with salt. Roast until tender, around 30–40 minutes. The beetroot should caramelise a little but not burn.

3. Place the onion, remaining oil and pinch of salt in a medium pan, cover with a lid and cook, over a very low heat for about 25–30 minutes, until very soft.

4. When the beetroot is tender and has cooled a little, roughly chop into small pieces and add to the onion with the caraway seeds, chilli flakes, sugar and vinegar. Simmer over a very low heat, uncovered, for around an hour, it should not burn or dry out but should cook down into a soft, sticky jam. Add a splash of water if needed. Taste for seasoning, remove from the heat and allow to cool.

5. I sometimes blend after cooking to a smooth purée, or it can be left as it is. Transfer to a container and store in the fridge for up to 3 weeks. The flavours settle after a day or two, although you can eat it straight away. Sprinkle with dill to serve.

JAMS AND SPREADS

PLUM AND FENNEL OVEN JAM

The oven is useful for making jam at the bakery but it is also true at home – one doesn't need to be hovering and agonising over a bubbling pan with this recipe. It might not be quite as perfect as traditional jam and needs to be stored in the fridge, but plums have a high proportion of pectin and so it will set fairly well. It has less sugar than a traditional jam so works as a compote on yoghurt for breakfast too, which is my favourite way to eat it.

MAKES 4 X 300ML (11 OZ) JARS

2.5kg (5½ lb) plums,
1–2 tsp fennel seeds, crushed in a pestle and mortar
600g (1 lb 5 oz) Demerara sugar

1. Preheat the oven to 180ºC/350ºF/gas mark 4. Line a deep baking tray with baking parchment.

2. Halve or quarter and destone the plums. Place on the tray and bake for 15–20 minutes or until they start to collapse.

3. Reduce the oven temperature to 150ºC/338ºF/gas mark 2 and sprinkle the fennel seeds and sugar over the plums.

4. Bake for 40–60 minutes, until the jam is bubbling all over with small, regular bubbles. Carefully stir a couple of times during baking to cook the jam evenly. Remove from the oven and, when cool enough to transfer, pour into clean, sterilised jars (see page 205). Cover with wax discs and add the lids. Set aside to cool completely then store in the fridge for up to 3 weeks.

RED ONION MARMALADE

I think this recipe originally came from the *Evening Standard* some time in the early noughties when instead of taking screen shots of endless recipes or ideas on my phone and then losing them as I now do, I used to cut them out and keep them in a folder for reference. There were some proper gems and I learned a lot from the *Evening Standard* and weekend newspaper supplements in the days when I had the time to read the papers for pleasure on weekend mornings. I have made it many times since then, usually from memory so it changes a little each time. Vary the herbs to taste or leave them out all together, it's all about the very slow cooking of the onions.

MAKES 600G (1 LB 5 OZ)

1kg (2¼ lb) red onions, peeled and thinly sliced in half moons
1 dried or fresh bay leaf
1 sprig fresh rosemary
2 sprigs fresh thyme
100g (3½ oz) red wine vinegar
150g (5 oz) dark brown sugar
salt and freshly ground black pepper

1. Place the onions and a pinch of salt in a medium pan, cover with a lid and cook, over a very low heat, for 30–40 minutes, until collapsed and very soft but without colour. Stir occasionally but otherwise leave them be.

2. Remove the lid from the pan and add the herbs, increase the heat to medium to allow some water to cook off and the onions to colour a little, about 10–15 minutes.

3. Add the vinegar and sugar and simmer until thick, for around 20–30 minutes, stirring frequently especially towards the end – it should be the texture of marmalade or jam. Remove from the heat and taste for seasoning – I like to add a little salt and plenty of black pepper at the end.

4. Try it in Blue Cheese and Red Onion Marmalade Twists (see page 96) or in cheese sandwiches.

RED ONION MARMALADE

SLOW ROASTED TOMATOES

I originally saw this recipe in a post by Carla Tomasi and immediately saw its potential for bakery use. Using the oven for food prep is a straightforward process but it also brings out the best from some very simple ingredients. I keep the technique but often change the herbs and seasonings. Below is an Italian version but I also like to make a Middle Eastern version with extra chilli, date syrup and coriander added after roasting. Garlic is a staple throughout both versions – cutting it in half and baking it cut-side down on the tray is one of my favourite shortcuts, it avoids the tedious task of peeling multiple cloves of garlic. The tomatoes are versatile and work particularly well in a sandwich with rocket and Provolone or stirred through pasta with Parmesan and basil.

MAKES 500G (1 LB 2 OZ)

1kg (2¼ lb) baby plum tomatoes
1 bulb garlic (try wet garlic)
2 red chillies
bunch of parsley
bunch of thyme
1 tsp sea salt
30g (1 oz) caster sugar
45ml (2 fl oz) olive oil
fresh basil leaves, to serve

1. Preheat the oven to 120ºC/250ºF/gas mark ½. Line a baking tray with baking parchment.

2. Cut the tomatoes in half long ways for some caramelisation or leave uncut for a juicier result. Cut the garlic in half through the centre of the cloves but leave the skin and stalk intact. Place cut-side down on the tray.

3. Layer the tomatoes, chillies and herbs on the tray, scatter over the sea salt and sugar and drizzle the oil over.

4. Roast for 2–3 hours, checking occasionally to make sure the tomatoes are drying and caramelising, but not burning. Turn the oven down if they colour too fast.

5. When roasted, set aside to cool a little, season to taste and remove the wilted herbs. Squeeze the garlic from its skin and stir into the tomato mix. Serve immediately, with fresh basil leaves. Or transfer to a container and refrigerate for up to 3 days but allow to come to room temperature before serving.

INDEX

ACKNOWLEDGEMENTS

This book came from the bakery and so it seems most appropriate to thank all of those who have worked at Margot and helped make it what it is today, without you all I could not have made this crazy idea become a reality. My architect Lucy Tauber and accountant Jane Capel – you are absolute stars. Marta, Richard, Alex, Hana, Laura, Joanna, Milena, Cesar, Daniel, Alvaro, Gianni, Daniele, Marina, Alysha, Samuel, Diana, Nicoletta, Jake, Juan, Raasikh, Ted and everyone else who has been part of the Margot story for a brief moment or for several years – thank you so much for your patience, enthusiasm and for all the early starts; you have taught me so much.

Thank you to our customers, many of whom have watched patiently as we found our way and endured and embraced the queues and the experiments; there are too many of you to name but I am so grateful to see familiar faces on busy days and I appreciate your support more than you can know.

Thank you to all the women who have made this book possible; to work with you all and watch you work together has been a great pleasure. Melissa, thank you for believing a book could be written by someone who had a bakery to run; Patricia, thank you – such a joy to see your generous and creative self in action. Charlotte, Rebecca, Cerys, Jessica, Rachel and Gizzi, your experience, vision and patience has made my foray into the world of publishing much easier than it would otherwise have been and I appreciate it so much. Anwen; I am so lucky to have you with me through this – a huge thank you for all your support and advice!

I think of the wonderful women behind the Margot name often; my Nana, Margaret (and my Grandad too!), thank you for always being there for me. And of Perlette who we miss greatly and speak of often. Thank you, Mum for letting me bake by your side – see what you started! Derek and Kevin, you are far away but never far from my thoughts. Victor, you never once doubted me and to have your unwavering confidence as I opened a bakery and then wrote a book too, thank you, it means everything. Rafael and Phineas; I work and bake and write and dream because I want you to know anything is possible. Keep being interested in everything, questioning everything. It is my greatest privilege to watch you grow and learn (and eat) and this book is for you, with all of my love.

Brimming with creative inspiration, how-to projects and useful information to enrich your everyday life, Quarto Knows is a favourite destination for those pursuing their interests and passions. Visit our site and dig deeper with our books into your area of interest: Quarto Creates, Quarto Cooks, Quarto Homes, Quarto Lives, Quarto Drives, Quarto Explores, Quarto Gifts, or Quarto Kids.

First published in 2019 by White Lion Publishing,
an imprint of The Quarto Group.
The Old Brewery, 6 Blundell Street
London, N7 9BH,
United Kingdom
T (0)20 7700 6700
www.QuartoKnows.com

Text © 2019 Michelle Eshkeri
Copyright © 2019 Quarto Publishing plc

Michelle Eshkeri has asserted her moral right to be identified as the Author of this Work in accordance with the Copyright Designs and Patents Act 1988.

All rights reserved. No part of this book may be reproduced or utilised in any form or by any means, electronic or mechanical, including photocopying, recording or by any information storage and retrieval system, without permission in writing from White Lion Publishing.

Every effort has been made to trace the copyright holders of material quoted in this book. If application is made in writing to the publisher, any omissions will be included in future editions.

A catalogue record for this book is available from the British Library.

ISBN 978 1 78131 876 8
Ebook ISBN 978 1 78131 877 5

10 9 8 7 6 5 4 3 2 1

Commissioning Editor Melissa Hookway
Designer Rachel Cross
Cover Designer Paileen Currie
Editors Charlotte Frost and Cerys Hughes
Photographer Patricia Niven
Production Controller Robin Boothroyd
Publisher Jessica Axe

Printed in China

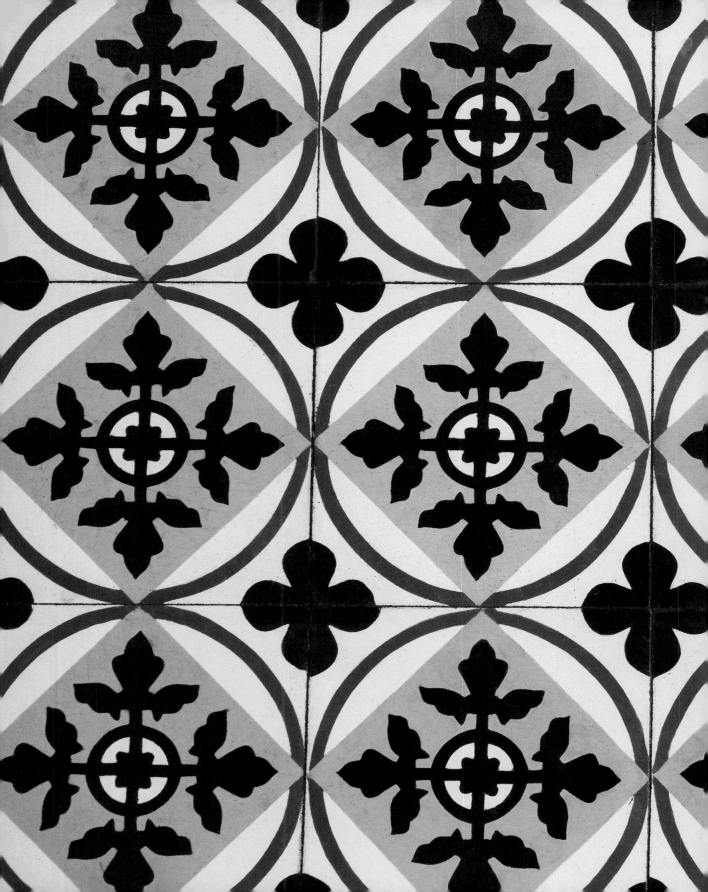